Our Heavenly Father
The Immutable Holy God

Steven Miller

OUR HEAVENLY FATHER THE IMMUTABLE HOLY GOD

iUniverse books may be ordered through booksellers or by contacting:

*iUniverse
1663 Liberty Drive
Bloomington, IN 47403
www.iuniverse.com
844-349-9409*

ISBN: 978-1-6632-3967-9 (sc)
ISBN: 978-1-6632-3968-6 (e)

Print information available on the last page.

iUniverse rev. date: 05/19/2022

CONTENTS

DEDICATION

I first want to thank my Savior, Jesus Christ, for His willingness to sacrifice His life on the cross, so I can have an assured eternal salvation.

I want to dedicate this book to my cherished wife, Kim. Thank you for being my bride for 40 years. I am thankful that I can traverse this life with you. It has not always been easy, but there is no one I would rather share the journey with.

To our three children; Jillian, Katelin and Christopher. Thank you for loving me as your dad. Your childhood passed too quickly, but it was the best part of my life.

Lastly, our grandchildren; Donovan, Daylen, Beckett, Quinn, and our coming baby G.

Hopefully, this list will grow.

FOREWORD

Some people have a calling to write a book. Steven G. Miller was called to write this one. You will find a straightforward answer to Salvation, the simplicity of the cross and the Holiness of our Lord and Savior Jesus Christ. He uses his apologetic gift to explain why all roads do not lead to heaven. He will prompt you to think deeper and to take you deeper into the logical cogent arguments as to the Truth of the Gospel message. He is not just another person with deeply held religious beliefs. You will discover that his world is anchored in years of research to seek and find the true meaning of life, the God given purpose and meaning for existence. I have known Steve for more than 50 years. Our paths crossed again in the early 80's where we served in the Criminal Justice System. He is a man of great integrity as he reveals his own transparency in pursuit of the answers for life. I know you will find this reading as I did, thought provoking and a prompting to search deeper to the reason for existence, trusting that you will find it at the foot of the cross where Christ will reach out to you with loving arms and say "come follow me". "For I am the way the truth and the life. No one comes to the Father except through me." John 14:6 NIV

Robert G. Toles

This is not an implied endorsement by any of our places of employment (Former or present), associations, boards or any other organization having been affiliated with.

INTRODUCTIVE THOUGHTS

I imagine there are a lot of people who desire to write a book. It could be their life journey they want to share with the readers, some learning they think is paramount for others to know, or some spiritual insights they think is worth expounding upon. In my case all three are somewhat true. I have been on a journey for over 35 years studying Christian theology, and now, I have a message I want to share about the implication of the Christian faith being true. So I am writing a book. Whether what I wrote is worth reading is up to the reader. I believe it will be worth your time, if you are willing to continue on into the substance of what I want to share? But it takes an investment, because I believe the book gathers steam as it progresses. I start the early chapters by laying the foundation for points to be developed later. The building of one principle upon another. As I develop a number of main themes, I keep returning to the central point, which is the imperative need to know the absolute holiness of our Heavenly Father. This comprehension opens our minds to the wonders of our eternal salvation, hence the emphasis of the implications of verse 6 in chapter 14, of the Gospel of John

There is simply no more preeminent subject than understanding God's loving plan for the redemption of mankind. But to really grasp the significance of this requires a knowledge of God's immutable holiness. Not exactly a common subject in today's Christian thinking. Most books are about the experience of the faith. What the faith means to them in their daily Christian walk. But something crucial is missing if the faith is limited to the experience of the faith. There are truths regarding God's nature that need to be explored, and understood, to grasp the true significance of the faith. So I want to share my spiritual journey with the hope that it will cause you to reconsider the real significance of the Christian faith.

For many years, I have been engaged in Christian deliberation, contemplating aspects of what I believe. Overtime, it became abundantly obvious to me that if the Christian faith is really true, the ramifications were far more significant than is being manifested by the average believer. We are exploring eternal issues. Those timeless truths and the eternal ramifications which are inherently implied, by the faith. For example, there are facets of Christianity that are very comforting, the love of God is one. And there are Biblical truths that are terrifying, Hell as another example. Those two concepts are hard to reconcile in our minds. They are tied up in the very essential nature of God Himself. The issue becomes even more complex when we remember that God is also immutable. That is, He cannot change, it is His intrinsic eternal nature. There never was, or ever will be, any aspect of God's nature that will change. He is eternally perfect in those attributes. With this in mind, I hope on this journey, to walk through the explorations of God's immutable nature. With the goal of gaining a better understanding of what those attributes should mean to us. And to lay out a logical thought process that resonates the significance of the Christian faith being utterly true. The idea being, if the Christian faith is really true, then we need to reconsider the implications, and those resulting eternal ramifications. If we are able to grasp the full connotations of the faith, it should lead us to evaluate how we are living in light of eternity.

Therefore, I intend on using a contrasting style that looks at the implications of Christianity being true, or not true. This is similar to some of the writing styles of Proverbs. Where thoughts are contrasted in some verses, and similar truths are parallel in other verses. Please keep that in mind throughout the reading of the book. And just like a good coach who teaches the fundamentals of a sport, I draw repeated attention to the key themes of this book. I don't want this study to be like a Sunday sermon that is preached only to be too quickly forgotten. So I repeat the major themes over and over to instill them into our memory. As an example, if the scriptures make a mention of a certain truth, it is fully true, even if only mentioned once. Think for a moment of the verses; John 3:16 or Ephesian 2:8-9. Either one alone would show the one condition to receive eternal life/salvation is to whomever believes the gospel. That truth would therefore be fully true even if only mentioned once. However, the gravity of salvation by faith alone, is so important, that, while much of the Bible is written to believers, over 150x in the New Testament, the one condition to receive the gift of salvation, is faith/belief/trust alone. This is particularly true in the Gospel of John, which is the only book of the Bible that is written to bring unbelievers to salvation. (John 20:30-31)

Ironically, one day as I was close to finishing up the final rewrites of this book, I was thinking about my three favorite books in both the Old and New Testaments. And I realized that this book of mine, was for a greater part, a summation of these six books. My favorite three books in the Old Testaments are; Genesis which starts the process that describes the greatness of God. The almighty one. The cause of everything. The Creator. Or, as He describes Himself, I Am who I AM. (While the actual descriptive term is first used in Exodus 3:14, the foundation for the concept starts in Genesis) By using this description of Himself, God is meaning self-existent without another cause. Next would be the book of Proverbs. The divine inspired wisdom, which when applied, teaches us how to live wisely. And then the book of Ecclesiastes. The folly of trying to live a purposeful life without a God focused understanding of life. The vanity of terrestrial life. In the New Testament; the Gospel of John. Christ is the one. The only source of salvation. The God/man who is the Savior of the world. The basis and foundation of giving freely, eternal life. The One who is the cornerstone of everything written about in the Bible. In the OT everything looked forward to Him. In the Gospels, this is Him. The balance of the New Testament, the significance of Him. Next in my list would be 1st Corithians. The highlighting of the temporal, and some of the eternal consequences, that will be manifested in how we live out the faith. Where the Bema Seat of Christ is explored, and the ultimate accountability of our lives is revealed. Then as the book continues, the significance of the resurrection is explored. In addition to these crucial teachings, Paul includes some warnings about the implications of sin in the life of the believer, the consequences of living contrary to the revealed will of God. And lastly, the book of Hebrews, which highlights the One who is greater than all. There is no one, nor any belief system, that compares to the majesty of the Lord and Savior. It is Him or no other. To draw back from Christ is to depart from the greatest person to have ever lived. To adhere to any other system of beliefs or religion, is meaningless in comparison. I believe if you are willing to stay with me, the journey will be worth the effort, as we see the theology of these six books of the Bible disseminated. Later, I realized, it is not limited to these six primary books. There are very significant theological truths from other books like; Galatains, Ephesians, Philippians and James, that are highly utilized too. This is because they forward the purpose of the book. James emphasizes putting one's faith into action. Galations stresses that we keep the absolute freeness of the gospel in the forefront of every gospel presentation. The books of Ephesians and Philippians give crucial theological truths. Therefore, while the first six are used as the primary theology, all ten, and a few more, are blended into prominence. These are some of the essential theological truths that I believe need to be revisited, and brought back into the minds of modern day Christians.

As with most people, we write like our personality. In this case, you will see that I am drawing out far-reaching truths of the Chrstian faith, without getting into the weeds of details. Making the central points the main points. But emphasizing them repeatedly to establish them solidly in our minds. However, this is not really a book on how to, but why these truths are so indispensable to living a life that is eternally relevant. By exploring the implications of the Christian faith actually being true, we answer those ultimate questions about what we profess to believe, and why it is so eternally significant. Those resulting answers should motivate us to be authentic life changing believers. If you are unsure if you even want to read this book, may I suggest reading a few select chapters, such as chapters; 3, 8, 9, 10, 11, or some of my concluding thoughts. I believe if you read a few of these selective chapters, you will want to engage with the rest of the book, because I believe the book grows in strength as it develops the central themes. By starting at the beginning, you will get the logical flow of the thought process that resonates with the importance of this subject.

Disclaimer of originality

One of the aspects of writing a book is trying to give credit to those so deserving. No knowledge is gained in a vacuum. There have been many helpful theological influences that contributed to the themes of this book. The difficult issue with this book is that most of the foundational material comes from schools of theology. Where hundreds, even thousands, hold the same views and have articulated those teachings, thereby giving credit to just one is most difficult. Since these theological views are held by the vast majority of those who have studied in those schools, therefore, most of what I have written is simply applying the natural inferences of the theology. I am focusing on aspects of Christian theology that I believe are not being cultivated adequately by most Christians. At least by the majority of Christians sitting in the pews on Sunday mornings. I am arguing that those truths are far more eternally significant than we appreciate. This effort of mine, is with the desired hope, that these truths would produce an awakening of our lethargic Christian lives. A more unmistakable response by believers, to a lost and dying world, one that is more focused on the eternal.

So please forgive me, if I have not properly given every credit where it is due. There is always a fear that one may have read or heard something, and not recall the origin of the idea. I hope that I have gathered a plethora of thoughts and truths, and developed them into those points of emphasis, that serve the message I want to communicate. You will see in my recommended reading at the end of the book, the many sources that I have studied and drawn insight from, but there are countless more. These theological truths that I am communicating are widely held within those schools that teach Free Grace salvation.

My mission to show the implications of the immutability of God's Holiness

Therefore, the intent of the book is to take those theological concepts, and then evaluate the significance of those truths. I then argue that there should be a more resolute response because Christianity is true! That our faith is far more eternally significant than is being practiced by most Christians. That in light of the temporary nature of life, our focus needs to be more on the eternal. It is like the stages of a jury trial. My reasonings are like the final arguments of a trial. (Not that I am alleging my book is the final say on these matters it just makes a good illustration) Like the facts from a trial which then are argued to show the relevance of the evidence. The arguments (this book) is attempting to communicate that the truths contained in the Chrisitan faith are the most crucial truths ever given to mankind. If the fundamentals of the faith are true, then it means....

Prayfully, this study will cause all readers to evaluate the significance of God's immutable and perfect holiness. For the unsaved, to grasp their dire condition before an immutable holy God, who must exact perfect justice to remain true to Himself. This with the hope they embrace the simple offer of God's redeeming love in the sacrificial death of Jesus Christ. For the believer, to have bold confidence, because they understand their secure salvation that is in Christ, because of the trustworthy promises of God. Which then results in moving forward in courageous faith, living a victorious life that is eternally significant, because we are already victorious in Christ. For the church, the body of Christ, to highlight again the reasons why we need to recapture the urgency for evangelism, and then discipleship, as our primary mission. And for both the individual believer and church, to grasp a deeper understanding of the implications of the faith, so often ignored, so that in a hundred years, long after we are gone from this world, our faith made a lasting difference. All this with the goal that we develop into mature, well grounded, and duplicating believers.

That in light of God's absolute immutable holiness, we are equipped with an accurate understanding of the gospel, so we are able to bring the lost to saving faith, then help disciple them into maturity. So please venture with me. While this is a bit of a long clumsy start, I believe if you continue on you will find what is written, worthwhile. Some thoughts about the Christian faith that are worthy of serious pondering.

Note: I truly believe that this book could have been better written if I used editorial help. I thought long and hard about having someone, or a few more gifted writers, polish up the readability of the book. I recognize that I am not a skilled writer, as you will see. You will likely find numerous grammatical errors, like words that should be capitalized and others that should not be. You will also notice that the flow of thought is not those of a skilled writer. I realize those deficiencies, but what is important to me is not my writing skill, but the urgent message I felt compelled to write.

Nonetheless, since I wanted to own the content of what I have written, to be a book of my spiritual journey into these essential truths, I am submitting it as I wrote it. Not a professionally written book, but a book from the heart. I believe the book starts slowly with some necessary principles, then gets more substantive, as we dig deeper into the content. It is like a movie that starts slowly, but details that did not seem so significant in the beginning, become crucial as it develops.

CHAPTER 1

Reason for writing

Why write a book about such a deep subject? It does not fit with today's mindsets. In days prior, these deeper subjects were often diligently studied by seasoned Christians. They thought more deeply on the inherent nature of God. They read the Bible with diligence to explore these deeper truths. Society has changed. We are now the entertainment and television generation. We are experientially based in our religious practice. We gravitate towards feeling good upon leaving a worship service. We want practical preaching that helps with living in a fast paced and stressful world. The normative desired Christian experience is the experience itself. How one feels about the practical daily aspects of their faith. Is it helpful for daily living? No need to get into the deep waters of theology. It is often very divisive anyways, and generally avoided in most churches.

Consequently, I believe there is a deficiency within the body of Christ, when we fail to comprehend some of the deeper truths about God. I am contending that until we grasp the true significance of who God is in His very nature, His eternal essence, the practice of our faith will lack an emphasis on what is eternally significant. Thereby, resulting in omissions regarding the implications of our faith. When this is the mindset, we will see the faith more as spiritual self-help, than eternally redemptive.

This is due primarily to our failure to grasp the enormous significance of the immutable holy nature of God. Perhaps, the most significant attribute of God, and this attribute is thoroughly described in the scriptures. When this is understood, those aspects of God's justice are understandable, and it reveals the reason for the administration of obligatory justice, that satisfies

His inherent righteousness, and relates to both time and eternity. This is intertwined with His natural desire to express His loving kindness to us, the undeserving. Both truths that coexist without compromising either His absolute immutable holiness or His loving kindness.

Much of what I am writing is part of my personal journey. For many years I grappled with aspects of the Christian faith. Finding assurance I was truly, and permanently saved, was always in the forefront of my thinking. How could there be an eternal Hell was a close second. I struggled with these and other aspects of my faith. Even to the point that I had considered just abandoning the faith. I was frustrated and feeling like my efforts to resolve these issues were leading to a fruitless end, at least early on in the journey.

Over time, I found insights that I believe answered my spiritual quest. I have not mastered them as a scholarly theologian, as I am self-taught. In that, I did not obtain an advanced degree in systematic theology, although, I do believe that after many years of diligent study from many valuable resources, has helped tremendously. In a sense, I would consider myself as having been trained by Dallas Theological Seminary, even though I never took a single class there. I have gravitated to those who were educated and/or taught there. It is not limited to DTS, since those trained at other schools holding the same essential theology were also largely used. This long and diligent pursuit of Biblical understanding helped equip me with a solid theological foundation, for which to think through these difficulties. It was a long, diligent step by step process, and it continues....

The essential beginning of the journey necessitated coming to a confident belief that the Christian faith was based on solid evidence. Included in this process was an assessment of some other faith traditions. Did they offer any solid evidence to substantiate their beliefs? From the beginning of my faith journey, I did not want to blindly assume my faith was true without first probing into other faith traditions. Once reasonably satisfied that Christianity was based on solid evidence, this journey continued in the process of better understanding what the scriptures taught. Often this process was simultaneously being pursued. The reading and studying of numerous Christian theology books, and reading the Bible over and over, was all part of the process of learning essential theological truths. Those truths contained in the scriptures, once better understood, allowed me to think through some of these difficult questions. This led ultimately to my contemplating the logical implications of Christianity. What does it mean if what we believe is really true? This is the major focus of this book. Who is God in His very essence and why that matters.

Let me make some acknowledgments before going deep into my presentation. First, this is not a book on evidence for God's existence or the apologetics for the Christian faith. Truth be told, I am simply inadequate to address those themes. There are far more capable people that should be read on those subjects. (Some of those resources are included in the recommended reading section)

Secondly, I am taking the Bible as the authority for my theme and teachings. I am asking you to assume these two truths for the purpose of what I am presenting in this book. First, there is a God. Secondly, he has spoken to us throughout the pages of the Bible. I acknowledge that if either of those two are flawed, then everything I write is pointless. To be sure the second assumption is dependent on the first. Should you personally wrestle with either of those two subjects? Then please take advantage of some of the suggested books or resources, as noted, they are found at the end of the book. They will be broken down in different categories. A study of those resources will affirm that I am on solid ground to assume both of these for the purpose of this book. There are other issues that I will not pursue. There is the study of epistemology, which is the study of the means of arriving at truth. How do we come to believe, what we believe, is reliably true? This too is often included in the study of apologetics. As noted, these shall be left for better informed writers to explain.

When referencing scriptural principles, I intend on giving my general summation of the Biblical concept, rather than an exegetical breakdown, or direct quotes. I am trying to make simple logical deductions of what the Bible teaches. Always asking, since the essential truths of the Bible are true, what are the implications? What does it mean by being true? As you will see, I follow the model of Jesus, and ask questions to illicit thoughts. As we progress, those truths are illuminated, as we apprehend the nature of God. What I have learned over the course of many years of study, I hope and pray, can be of value for your walk with our Lord, and a renewed motivation to live a Christian life that is honoring our Lord. With this understanding, we would leave behind some of our trivial temporal pursuits, and exchange them for ones that are more eternally consequential. Living a life that leaves an eternal legacy.

With this background, let's focus on this journey into truths that are foundational for what we need to believe about God, and why it matters. You will see recurring themes that emphasize God's holiness, God's love, mankind's sinfulness, the master plan of God's redeeming love, and the consequences of how we live out our faith. I hope to show that the implications of those truths are far more eternally significant than what is being experienced in our personal lives, and in most of our local bodies of believers. I plan on taking these chapters in a progressive and logical order of thought. The building of one truth that leads to the logic of the next, to arrive at some conclusions, that makes better sense of the whole Christian experience. Therefore, there are ideas woven throughout the book that should cause both the unbeliever and believers to wrestle with the logical implications of the Christian faith. While it is assumed that Christianity is true for the purposes of this book, I want to walk through the thought process, as though you are evaluating the significance of the Christian faith for the first time, but not in a traditional apologetics frashon. The desire is to look at the Christian faith afresh, so as to see the actual implications of being true. Let's start the journey in logical order.

CHAPTER 2

The journey

With this introduction, let's step back and start this thought process in its logical order, at least as I experienced this journey of mine. I think this is valuable since many will identify with this journey. It started with an epiphany of sorts. I remember one day many years ago I was thinking about the Christian faith. I am sure it was more of a process but one day in particular stands out to me. I remember sitting in church thinking about the Christian faith. This thought is not the most profound thought ever to have passed through the mind of mankind. It was simply; what if Christianity is not even true? A simple deductive thought. Most of us have entertained that thought. This question could apply to either Christianity or any religious belief. I suspect we all question our beliefs at times. It may even be good to question our faith, since the process should lead to a stronger confidence in our faith, or reveal to us that what we are believing is not sustainable by the evidence. Therefore, for the Christian, this evaluation will reveal that there is strong evidence for the Christian faith. In that case, the process can be very helpful. (Obviously, if Christianity is true, then there is a God) In my situation, on that morning, I was asking myself why I was spending my Sunday mornings in Church? I was very young in the faith. Actually, I am quite sure I was not a born again Christian, I was a culturally Christian, but questioning the faith. In my mind, I was unsure if it was even true. I was mentally wrestling with the logical implications of being really true or simply a cultural tradition. This thought that Sunday morning provoked a series of thoughts that led me on this journey.

I recognized that there were numerous religious traditions in this world. I was simply asking myself why did I adhere to the Christian faith? Since it is true that most religious traditions are passed on within a culture. That is why certain religious traditions are grouped in particular societies or countries. I was therefore asking myself, if my faith tradition was believed to be true, simply because I was raised in the USA? It is unlikely I would believe what I was being taught, if I was born and raised in another county with another faith tradition. I realized that what I held as true could be nothing more than culturally held beliefs handed down, from one generation to the next. Furthermore, I was not seeing much substance or evidence, to convince me that there was much significance to the faith. A practice that helped people be better people. A tradition of values that made our society better. Cultural beliefs that gave unity to us as a country, but its true eternal significance seemed to evade me. And, when measured in light of eternity, it did not add up with what I was seeing. My thoughts were; if our faith was true, the significance and practice of the faith, was not being revealed in most of the personal lives of those I was sharing this worship experience with, or in the priorities of the churches. At least to the degree suggested by our declarations of the faith. My impression was, we were practicing a faith that lacked a genuine understanding of the implications of what we professed to believe.

These observations, begged me to ask myself, what evidence did I have that Christianity was even true? As noted, inherent within this question, is the God question. What is the significance of believing in the Christian God? This led to a tremendous desire to explore the validity of the Christian faith. I needed to know if it was based on any solid evidence. For without this confidence that the faith is built on verifiable evidence, why practice the Christian faith? Why am I even sitting in church? Why live a manner of life that does not always enhance my personal comforts or desired pleasures? Actually, I could surmise that my faith of that day did little more than make me feel guilty, so I would be a better person. And maybe a bit more compassionate and kind, but other than that?

I was mindful that it was a fruitless endeavor to adhere to the principles of the Christian faith, if there is no substantial and credible evidence to suggest that it is even true. (At least from the perspective I held on that day) While I acknowledge that there are secondary benefits for our society.

Maybe even some good self-restraining disciplines that provide stability for me individually, and protect me from foolish decisions, I was inclined to make. Those self-restraining inherent qualities of morality that emanate from Christian teachings, but no apparent critical benefits, unless, the essentials of the faith were dependability true. Then, in that case, the faith was of immeasurable value. These questions were part of the emotional and spiritual journey I was wrestling with early on in my quest of authentic faith.

So for over the last 35 years, I have studied and pursued this knowledge, in order to know the truthfulness of the Christian faith, and then understand the implications of being true. I certainly am not an expert, but the end results of that pursuit has led me to believe what I was taught to believe, is in fact true, although not as I was originally taught. And with that confidence that the essence of Christianity was true, caused me to realize that these truths are eternally significant. I discerned from the onset of this journey, that if Christianity is genuinely true, and it is! It is not being given the proper weight, either in the private lives of believers, or in the practice of the average local church. We are only a shadow of its reality. But I am getting ahead of the logical thought process.

It is fruitless to start a topic of this nature without first establishing a base significance for God's existence. It is the foremost question of all time. The answer to that question magnifies everything. It either affirms that we have preeminent value as created humans, or it diminishes the very significance for our existence. Should the question of God's existence be affirmed? That being true, then life has an intended meaning. It would affirm that we as the central part of God's creation must be paramount. Since there is no other created life that is created in the image of God. And that would mean our existence is consequential. Which would give hope for life beyond the present, if the message of the Bible is true, and trustworthy. Then, to that extension, there is assured eternal hope in the Christian Biblical Gospel, as I will explain as we proceed through the book.

The alternative is also true. A denial of God is ultimately a denial of hope and meaning. It is hard to argue we are significant in this universe if we are only a link in the chain of biological evolution. I conjecture that one could pursue pleasure or power or fame in an effort to have fleeting meaning. Many do so, endeavoring to achieve a particular recognition in the community. Those achievements could be in fashion or sports or financial success, or one of many other pursuits that lead to a desired community status. Only to realize in the waning years of life, that they were inadequate reasons to live. I suspect we all do so to a degree. We often look for the approval of man to give our lives perceived meaning. This is most often based on achieving some perceived social standing. For some, there is little limit to what they will not personally sacrifice, in order to achieve some perceived level of influence or social standing. Many will sacrifice what is truly meaningful, just to satisfy some felt deficiency in their life. This is generally because they fail to see the purposes that God has prescribed, as the means for a truly meaningful life.

But therein lies the perplexity of trying to live a meaningful life in a purposeless world. Many have achieved some of these personal quests. They sacrificed tremendously to achieve their desired societal goals, only to find it was ultimately unfulfilling. They are left with the reality that those achievements have lost their allure. The end result of these terrestrial pursuits is one is left with a realization of the insignificance of what was pursued and accomplished. Think of winning the World Series in baseball. To some, a grand personal achievement, a goal of a lifetime, to others, so what. They are indifferent to what some may feel was a grand personal accomplishment. In 20 years, the so what, is magnified. Few remember what you accomplished anyways. Those achievements are now, or will be, lost in the history of time. No matter how beautiful or successful or accomplished one is in sports, those moments of celebration are transitory and short-lived. We will age, lose our beauty, or physical abilities, only to be replaced by a new younger generation. Who then chase their dreams only to be later forgotten. Part of the theme of the book of Ecclesiastes in the Old Testament. The vanity of it all. This is the problem of existential living for those who do not share our faith, or even a belief in God. Ultimately, the achieved goal is meaningless.

Therefore, the obvious conclusion is; that living a life in a surmised Godless universe, undermines any foundation for values, purposeful living, and disavows any hope beyond the grave. If we come to this conclusion? It results in an obvious sense of meaninglessness. Hopelessness! A vaper in our time of history is all we are. Temporal pursuits that lead to nothingness. In light of eternity, the humanistic question one must ask; what was it all about? What was all for?

This is particularly the reason why this topic needs to be considered carefully. Everything meaningful in life is dependent on the answer to the God question. To take the thought a step further, it is also dependent on the personality of God. Because who God is in His essence is absolutely crucial. Is He inept and/or distant? Is He knowable? Does He care about me or my situation? Is He a good God? Does He care about justice? Does He love me? Does He offer any real hope for our lives beyond the grave? The questions could continue. How these are answered will reveal what we believe regarding the purposes of life. And how they are answered is dependent on who God is in His very essence. It will also permeate the practicalities of our Christian faith. If we understand God to be less than holy or loving or faithful or trustworthy or able, then there is no confidence to be had. His intrinsic nature is the cornerstone for everything we trust to be trustworthy. Because we have a dependable faith only if we have a dependable God!

Furthermore, rediscovery of those priorities are essential to our time in history, due to the moral decline. It is clear that many Christians and churches have abandoned the teaching of Biblical truths. They are habitually foreign to most of the present day Christian's mindsets. Whereas, while the truthfulness of the Christian faith has been strongly established, it is not being grounded in our daily priorities, or held with actual real significance. And that is essential to what I am trying to expounding upon. Since the truth of what I am writing is based on the truthfulness of Christianity, the inclusion of the study of apologetics is necessary if there is doubt to your faith. Even if you are not struggling with the truthfulness of the Christiain faith, it may be for someone with whom you want to share your faith, so we need to be prepared with solid reasons for why we believe.

However, as noted, traditional apologetics is not my focus. Once we come to the satisfying conclusion that Christianity is true, we need to move on to the implications of that truth. Therefore, we need to know the truth, then recognize that this truth is far more significant than is being portrayed by the body of Christ, we are living in the shadows of the faith.

Once we have come to reasonable comfort that our faith is strongly attested to by good evidence. The natural progression is to develop the next steps in the process; learning who is this God? Who is God in His essence? And then why does it matter?

It was also during this long process, that I found myself struggling with the priorities in our churches, and trying to grasp the insignificance of what was often being practiced. I was mentally processing how the present day preaching measures up in light of what the Bible teaches as the ultimate priority, one's eternal destination. This path returned to some of the difficult to understand, traditional orthodox teachings of Biblical truth, which led back to the concept of Hell. A circular process of which I had little understanding how this could all be reconciled. It did not make reasonable sense. How could Christians hold onto a doctrine that is so unconscionable. It was hard to accept how this could actually be true, at least in the beginning of this journey. (I will continue to wrestle with this notion throughout the book)

Some concluding thoughts on this chapter. All of this was dependent on knowing God's nature. This background is necessary to understand traditional doctrines of the faith. Those teachings that have lost their appeal to the modern-day Christians. The doctrines of the faith, which seem unattainable in our thinking, which then are ignored or abandoned. Those aspects of the faith that answer the big questions in life. How do we qualify for heaven? Is there an eternal hell? Will there be real justice? Does it really matter how I live out my Christian faith? And, can we have absolute assurance of personal salvation? To be sure, these were the big ones. To find satisfactory answers entails the knowledge of God Himself. Like any valuable relationship in our lives, knowing intimately the person is crucial. Can I have confidence, based on their character, that I can trust the person with my life and future? This is why the study into the nature of God is pivotal, especially for the Christian. The better we know our trustworthy Heavenly Father, the better we can cope with the difficulties of life, and have the assurance that our devotion is a reasonable act of service. The sacrifice of community status and/or our personal comforts, in order to make the gospel message known, is the most sensible activity to undertake. In a world of many conflicting voices, it is crystal clear that knowing the truth is more important than ever. The time we invest in coming to know God personally, is a worthy pursuit. These struggles were part of my journey of faith, and it all started many years ago, with the simple question; is it even true?

CHAPTER 3

The Ultimate Reality

Let's come to grips with an inescapable truth, we all will die one day! This is the one fact that is the most undeniable of all truths. It is the sobering recognition that our physical lives, when measured in light of eternity, are just a mist. Regardless of what we do or accomplish, it is temporary. I have never met a 200 year old man. This reality of the brevity of life is also reinforced by a simple trip past a cemetery. There, as represented by the tombstones, is the reminder that there is an inescapable limitation to our lives.

I have visited cemeteries back east on historical trips, and locally, viewing the graves of those long lost. I have stood at the graves of loved ones and pondered life, and its brevity. In many of those cemeteries back east are buried some very historical people. Those we read about in our history books. I have contemplated what life was like for them. Realizing that their lives were more than just history, they were as real as I am now. Undoubtedly, one day I will be joining them, I hope not too soon. In contemplating their lives, I wonder about how they live. The time in history in which they lived. Did they die for a cause like our freedom? Were they fortunate to enjoy the many blessings life can bring? Did they unjustly suffer? Did their lives include a lot of pain? Was their life an immensely positive impact to those who knew and loved them? Or, did they waste their lives in pursuit of fruitless and meaningless activities? Were they overtaken by the vices of life? Did they invest their lives in learning, so as to leave lasting lessons of wisdom, for their beloved family? The ponderings could continue.

It is also clear by reading the tombstones that many experienced very short lives. Never living long enough to have a family or experience the lasting love of family. Way too many children are buried there. Some gave their lives so we could have this freedom to write books or practice our faith. The speculations could continue. One thing is absolutely true, cemeteries are a sober reminder that life is temporary. Maybe something we all need to pause and consider, since it is in mine and your future. Sometimes we need a little reflection to put life back into perspective, because while death is a natural part of life, it is so final.

I remember a few years ago when I was approaching 60 years of age, it struck me that this journey of my life was starting to wind down. Let's say for argument's sake that I have a hopeful lifespan of 80 to 90 years. Should that be the case, then I was somewhere between 3/4 to 2/3 over with my life. Not only is that likely true, but the experience of life reminds us that the later days are most often those that include health challenges and loss. The time when we say goodbye to many good friends and family. To compound my reality with aging, I had read an article in Reader's Digest, that suggested that the best years of life were our fifties. If that was true? Then upon turning 60, the best years of my life were behind me. In reflection, I was realizing that there were desired goals that I would never achieve. As most men who enjoy sports, it was clear that I would never achieve greatness on the field or court. I still take pleasure in beating my buddy Bob in golf, but most dreams of athletic greatness were going to be adolescent dreams that would never be satisfied.

Even as a parent, I understood that chapters of my life had passed, and would never be recaptured. I remember when our last child was leaving for college. (Our daughters had already ventured out) I knew a change was occurring, and our life would never be the same. I sat in the backyard while my wife took our son to pick up some last minute supplies for college. (He was leaving the next day) I did not have a few tears, I sobbed. A tough realization that the day to day aspects of being a parent with children in the home had come to an end. A reminder of the end of so many good memories of them growing up. Their friends being in our home. The sporting events. The vacations we took as a family. The apple orchards. The meals and homework that are a normal part of most of our lives. It was a very abdicating feeling. The letting go of my central role as a dad.

I liked being a dad with children in the home. I would continue being a dad, but it would never be the same. I remember feeling that it passed so quickly. But also a reinforcing reminder to me, that everything in life had an ending point, the good ones, and those we would just soon forget.

As I pause and evaluate my life to that point in time, depending on my focus, I can surmise that my life was reasonably successful, or underwhelming. As with most lives, it was a mixture of both. I had moments that brought great joy and personal satisfaction. There were achievements that I can be proud of. There also were many choices, or actions, that left memories of regrets and remorse, those I wish to put behind me. Truth be told, all in all, life has been relatively good for me. I come from a solid family. We had our normal life struggles and hardships, but overall, I have lived a relatively quality life. My wife and I have three adult children. All three turned out establishing successful professional, and for the most part, meaningful personal lives. We are blessed with a number of grandchildren. (Hopefully that number will grow) We are fortunate that our children started having their children early, this is enabling us to enjoy quality time with them. The time to experience those joys of watching them traverse through their journey of life. Our grandchildren are fortunate that they have loving, devoted, and caring parents. But that does not surprise me, their mother modeled that well for them. She is a good person, and easy to be married to, I am thankful for that!

But I regressed, this is not about me, it is the reflection on life, for whatever it brings, it is temporary and fleeting. The inescapable fact is that life is temporary, and often contains more regrets and hardships than we had hoped. But certainly short in light of eternity! In a hundred years it will be doubtful that there will remain any significant memory of my life. Nothing will outlast me, other than the faith and values that I passed on, and lives impacted by my sharing of the gospel. (These principles will be developed as we progress through the book) (If you want to do a fascinating study. Do a study of the ancestry of Jonathan Edwards. The profound impact his life had. What legacy are you leaving?)

Recognizing the reality of this truth, should cause everyone to reflect, as I have been doing. It is clear that we all will one day experience death. We will step into the world of eternity. NO stopping its inevitable conclusion.

We are all going to die one day. For me, it was becoming clearer that this life is now starting to pass by, and I cannot stop the progression. Like most, I wish I could start over with what I have learned over the course of these years. There would be some choices that I would have avoided, nonetheless, life is a one way street, birth to death. As the shadows of my life slowly get darker and darker, I realize my time here on earth is not going to last in perpetuity.

The natural question, from a purely human perspective is to ask; if there is any reason for hope? Is there any reason to hold on to confidence that all our struggles and effort to make life meaningful, were not a fruitless effort? A mist that quickly passed with no ultimate purpose or reason. Is a destiny with the cemetery all we have to look forward to? So the obvious conclusion is that death is in my future, and sad to say, yours too! Regardless of how old you are, you will come to realize this journey is not going to last forever. We can deny it. We can ignore it. But it will come in its time. The inevitable truth, for everyone's life, is that it is temporary!

This should lead everyone who is not sure of their eternal destination, to consider the most terrifying question, what then? Are you sure? For those of us who are believers, and have the hope of the resurrection, a chance to reflect and make sure we are living eternally fruitful lives.

It is not just a God question, but who is God, and what has He revealed that gives us this hope? This is the journey we are taking in this book. Let's continue to establish some spiritual principles that will give this book journey real meaning.

CHAPTER 4

An illustration to demonstrate universal morals and unintended consequences of leaving Biblical truth

With these introductory thoughts and reflections, I want to continue to lay the foundations for the book. I hope to show in chapter four of this book, using an illustration, that some universal morals are generally agreed upon by the majority of society. That life needs to be lived in a moral universe. Even most atheists will acknowledge that they adhere to moral standards in their lives, even if they do not hold to a Christian worldview. Even if one does not ascribe to the authority of the Bible, people have traditionally practiced many of those values that emanate from what is taught in the Bible. For example, we can see even most atheists honor the bonds of marriage, a union established by God Himself. We also would agree that hurting a child for pure pleasure is morally wrong. The question in this chapter is the basis of our moral standards? Whose or what values are determinative? And, what does this mean to unbelievers and/or Christians? We all hold to moral values, but whose, and why?

I think you will find this forthcoming marital illustration rather absurd, but it does drive home some points that I want to make. Therefore, there are a few purposes for the illustration. One is to show that as a society we generally agree to commonly held community values. This is necessary or we would find life intolerable. Can you imagine for a moment living in a society having no standards? Where everyone individually determined what was right or wrong. Look at the societies that lost that moral foundation, the chaos that ensued.

Ordinarily, we live out these values without really thinking through the origin of why. We naturally adapt to those community standards to remain socially acceptable. In general, these community values are a benefit to society. Established values provide stabilization for the orderly functioning of society. These values provide for the healthy order of society, like the sanctity of marriage for one, and the natural protection of children is another. Even if one does not ascribe to the truthfulness of the Bible, those common values provide moral unity, and are a benefit to all of us. Furthermore, the higher principled values, like those that were held by most of our early founders of our country, gave the moral foundation for one of the greatest, and most prosperous countries in recorded history. And these are the same values inherent in the Christian faith. (See the website, Wallbuilders, for historical evidence for this statement) There is a necessary moral foundation that instills virtuous living, so individuals behave with self-restraint, and the need for forced compliance is less needed. This allows for the practical enjoyment of life we all want to experience. And as we progress in the book, we will see those foundational values need to be anchored in a foundation that is always true, and that is the eternal attributes of God. This concept will be developed as we progress in the upcoming chapters.

Consequently, there are unintended consequences when society slowly evolves away from the Biblically based, moral foundational principles. Therefore, when we leave this foundational highground, and we deviate from those Christian norms, we find that we have diminished our quality of life. When this is the progression, we see crime increase, families become unstable, substance abuse increase, and so forth. The progression of this thinking is devastating to society. We need the foundation of a moral anchor that is established by an objective standard. This is not achievable in a morally subjective society where each member determines what is right or wrong, as I will pontificate on as we continue.

In this illustration we will see the twin truths. First, is that we live in an acknowledged moral universe. I know it is not acceptable to walk down a street naked, even though it does not hurt anyone. And secondly, it will clarify the point that we need to understand God's immutable nature, so our morals are anchored to some standard that is always true. This is logical since God has established standards that emulate from His nature. The clear inference is that God's nature should be foundational for our personal lives, and be reflected as the standard for moral conduct in society. That is why God the Holy Spirit guided the writers of the scriptures to reveal His immutable perfect nature. So we can have our feet firmly planted on an everlasting foundation of truth. This truth is needed for both daily living, and as a determinative standard to evaluate the requirements to having a relationship with God. (Showing our need for salvation) The alternative is, we are left with our feet planted in midair, where all moral choices are formed by our own inherently sinful personal preferences. For those not holding to anchored values based on the intrinsic nature of God, we will see that the forthcoming illustration is both logical and acceptable, since in this view there are no transcendent values that define behavioral choices as either moral or immoral, it is up to each person to determine their own standards of morality.

Furthermore, we will see as we continue on in the book, that there are consequences to the violations of those standards, both in time and in eternity. If we accurately understand God's nature, we will see why God has prescribed, and described them for us, they are for our good and God's glory. (See Deuteronomy 10:13) They also show the unbeliever why they need a Savior, since their inability to measure up to God's standards, will highlight their need.

Additionally, should we as Christians practice the faith as intended, it will reflect God's nature in His children, so we as His children manifest our Heavenly Father to the world. It is the practice and not just the beliefs that manifest the benefits. (See the book of James) It is very apparent that our moral foundations are crumbling and this is being revealed in the brokenness of our society. We were once the hub of Christian truth. The great missionary country that sent out men and women to share the hope of the gospel and promote those Christian principles, now we are the hub of porngraphy, something has changed. A bit of a long winded introduction to set the stage for my illustration, but here is my illustration of the moral implications of what we believe.

Let's say a man has a wife he truly loves. He desires her happiness. She comes home one day and confesses she is infatuated with another man she knows from work. The husband, desiring her happiness, grants her permission to have a weekly relationship with this co-worker. So, once a week, she and her co-worker have a sexual encounter. At the end of that day she returns home and freshens up for dinner. They share a cup of coffee or a glass of wine, and discuss their days. They enjoy some companionship and a meal together. Later that night the two of them share a normal spousal relationship. The husband experiences a satisfying sexual experience. It could be even argued that this experience is enhanced because she brings new experiences to their bedroom. A more expressive sex life. Life goes on as normal.

It can be logically argued that the husband has not been harmed. His sexual experience had been enhanced. He has lost nothing monitiary. He still has the companionship of his wife. They share quality time together at the end of the day. He was not physically harmed, nor personally deceived, since he willingly granted his permission. Even if it was argued he was harmed, how is it determined? There is no basis of morality to claim he has been harmed, or been cheated of his marital benefits, since in this perspective there are no objective divine standards, in which to qualify a marriage as a uniquely sacred union. It is simply a relationship agreement both find acceptable. They enjoy the benefits of the relationship without the normal exclusive sexual standards found in traditional marriages. Almost like friends with benefits concept. In this illustration, there is nothing that makes this relationship arrangement immoral, if there is no God! This is the logical and deductive result of denying the moral values that flow from the revelation of God's immutable holy nature. This is what society is presently doing, by removing the anchor of our moral foundations, which is God Himself, thereby, claiming most all expressions of sexuality are acceptable. But is it?

However, should we affirm the reality of God and His nature, then the relationship agreement is absurd! He has spoken. And He has clearly revealed His desire and purpose for marriage. Consistent with the belief in God, and an understanding of His design for traditional marriage, we can see the incongruous marriage arrangement portrayed in the illustration. This is why we need to think through these questions. It conveys whether marriage is sacred and has God given purpose, or subject to being redefined by society. Even what constitutes a marriage. That is why these progress steps need to be thought through. Think through this progression of reasoning to determine the foundation for morality. 1. Is there a God? 2. Has He revealed His nature? 3. Has He spoken in a particular book? 4. What are the purposes for what He has spoken? 5. What does this teach us about how we are to live? 6. What are the consequences for how we live? 7. What are the eternal consequences of what He has said? This is why understanding the very nature of God is so essential to everyday life.

This is not just some theological argument, it has very practical ramifications too. At the very least, it will show the absurdity of living with indistinguishable values that are driven by the ethics of this world, and not by the anchor of God's nature. Everything we conjecture about this illustration reflects the basis of our values. Whether we hold to divinely revealed values, or subjective and emerging values of culture. What we hold as the true foundation for our morals, will determine our view of the sanctity of marriage, and the foundations for all our morality. Let's continue looking at the logical implications of the illustration. The evolving negative consequences of deviating from God's standards.

We can see these changes in our society as illustrated through a few mental pictures. A few years ago my wife and I were dog and cat sitting for our son and his wife. One evening we went downtown for some ice cream. There in the parlor was a picture, of what I surmised to be the opening of the ice cream parlor, an old black and white picture. What particularly interested me was that all the men had dress jackets on and every woman wore a dress. I remember appraising the time and culture of when the picture was taken. Jump forward in time and recall the television show, I Love Lucy. A period that was likely somewhat close to the taking of this picture. If you recall seeing the bedroom? They were a married couple and had a son. What is striking is that the bedroom scene contained two separate beds. It was not appropriate to show a single bed even though they were married. It was reported that it was even unacceptable in those days to mention that she was pregnant on the show, even though they were married. Jump forward to many of the popular shows we now watch. The casualness of sexual relationships of those who are unmarried, and how normal we now accept that as the changing community standard. Jump forward again, and think of the impact of the internet age. The disturbing statistics on pornography viewing, even among Christians, and sadly, Pastors. What has happened to us and our country? How did we drift so low in such a short time? To the point we hold few things as sacred anymore. This is part of the journey of this book. Regardless whether you are a Christian or not, it is clear something has gone astray. We are abandoning our trustworthy anchor which results in losing our moral bearings.

Others, who do not hold our values, will ask if our drift is really an issue. They will assert that the problem is those restrictive traditional beliefs. Some will even argue that we as a society are making progress by freeing ourselves from outdated Christian beliefs. A freeing of our sexual expressions, without the unneccesary restrictions, imposed by the expectations of the Christian faith. But those perceived benefits are not affirmed by any reasonable assessment of our crumbling society. The evidence is clear that crime is skyrocketing, divorce rates have grown exponentially over the last hundred years, more and more children are born out of wedlock, drug abuse is rampant, and there is an overall decline of our mental health. Furthermore, our children are struggling as never before, with declining academic proficiency, and socially, because of the brokenness of their world. Their very innocence is being stolen by this progressive thinking, and is accelerating due to the promotion of very sexual expressive material to young children in some schools. These descriptive examples are the byproduct of the removal of the inherent, self-restraining, character building morality, contained in our Christian heritage. Let's return to the purpose of the illustration, the need for anchored truth.

Regardless of the acceptance of our changing society, God has not changed. He is who He is, and He cannot change. We have a moral conscience that is either formed by secular society, or is based on Biblical revelations. We anchor to one or swim with the other. One is a sure foundation, and the other is a devaluing of our morality, to the point that life itself, eventually becomes so devalued, that little is cherished. The stripping of our anchor from our long held Biblical foundation has profound consequences. It is the loss of our moral glue that once gave society stability. This forsaking view of Biblical morality, that formerly built our conscience, is being sheared from our virtuous foundation by the media, entertainment and culture. This promotion of freedom away from our righteous moral foundations, by the Godless secular left, is not producing the real freedom promised. The redefining truth to avoid guilt does not resolve the feelings of guilt, it only suppresses it. It only gives them the freedom to act with fewer inhibitions of their unrestrained carnal nature. (Romans chapter 1) The natural solution is a return to the faithful practice of the Christian faith. The life renewing hope of the Gospel. (As explored in chapter 27) A true righteous foundation our country needs, the resetting of what is believed, with what is truth.

Therefore, the question of which foundation we build our values on, is all dependent on whether there are immutable truths. As the drift from objective truth grows, and Biblical truth is removed as the foundation for our society, and our personal lives, we see the organic consequences. The very fabric of personal and societal life comes unraveled. Even a superficial observation of our society makes this clear. So does the changing from dresses to pornography hightlight how rapid we have transgressed the moral landscape. Where the Speaker of the United States Representatives proposed rules in the House, that personal pronouns cannot be used, because it is offensive to those who do not hold to traditional Biblical truth, and we casually accept it without too much pushback. Regardless of this evolving movement, I treasure being a son, a husband, a dad and a brother. I am not adopting those emerging values simply because that is the drift of our culture. God created males and females. Only the absurd denies that there is no difference and people can choose their sex. The science is absolutely clear, no one can change their X or Y. It gets to the point that the argument for choice of sex identity is just ridiculous. I feel compassion for those who are caught in the confusion of our moral decline, but it is like the person who said we are a society with our feet firmly planted in mid air, anchored to nothing.

We should grant that the illustration could be logically valid, the determinative factor is not only is there a God, but also what is His nature. There is a growing lack of understanding of who God is in His essential nature. Those truths which determine my values and code of conduct, are based on how we understand the revealed nature of God. Has He spoken in the pages of the Bible? I hope to illustrate in the pages of this book that a belief in God's existence, when affirmed, shows it has both temporal and eternal significance. That there are consequences for the violations of His standards. While different, there are inherent consequences for both the Christian and nonbeliever. There are implications of those truths that determine our eternal destiny, that give meaning and foundational values to every life, and to every aspect of life.

So let's explore in more detail why we need to examine the revelation of God, understand what He has said, believe it, and then put it into practice. In the pages of this book we will continue to explore aspects of God's nature and how that is interconnected with our lives. Not only the practical aspects in this life, but by far, the eternal consequences. You will notice that many of my thoughts are reiterated repeatedly. That is intentional. The purpose is to drive home these truths so we reflect on the implications of God's immutable holy nature. I do not want to breeze over what is intended to be far-reaching truths. I want to keep refocusing on these essentials. The anchor of truth.

CHAPTER 5

The basis of truth

The investment of your time learning essential and indispensable Biblical truth is absolutely necessary to be anchored. We all need to know what we believe, but also why. We have a crisis of Biblical ignorance in the Western church and that to our shame! We have the resources available to us, like nobody has ever enjoyed, but our anchor is only as strong as we are grounded in that truth. It is hard to live eternally meaningful lives, if we do not grasp the central emphasis of what the Biblical writers have passed on to us in the pages of scriptures. We tend to read more emotionally satisfying material that helps with our emotional or spiritual struggles. Hoping to find the illusion of the cosmetic life, that is just that, an illusion, more so than the substantive teachings that we have historically professed to believe. Those anchored eternal truths, for which we will be held accountable one day. The undeniable truth is, that eternity is a long long time, and this life is undeniably short. But it is not limited to those eternal destiny truths. We have drifted from those anchoring truths that give foundational principles for all our moral decision making. In the absence of absolute truth, we live life without ultimate purpose. We also lose our ability to leave a God honoring legacy, which is being exchanged for temporal pursuits of pleasure.

Therefore, it is essential that we are equipped, so our lives are eternally meaningful. There is a difference. The former is being equipped with the knowledge of truth. It is hard to be fruitful, if we do not know what the scriptures teach regarding vital Biblical truth. The latter is, once understood, are we motivated to put to use? To be eternal difference makers, since we now better understand the gravity of what is true. This is what James, our Lord's younger half brother, wrote about in his book. He criticized them for looking into the mirror and quickly forgetting their face. They knew the truth, but they were quick to set it aside. They were not putting it to practical use. This is a point I am trying to make, if our faith is well established and true…. Let's continue.

We now need to move on to consider the implications of some of the more essential truths that the Bible illuminates. Those eternal verities that we naturally shy away from. These implications should be entirely anticipated if we accurately perceive God's nature, if we know God's essential nature, His immutable and infinitely perfect nature! Therefore, this exploration of divine truth, is a process of coming to know God Himself. In particular, the comprehension of our God, who is immutable holy. I believe if we as a people of God would contemplate the implication of what we profess to believe, it would change how we live, and anchor our lives in the eternal. But that process will not take place until we take the time to know God as He has revealed Himself. Not as He has been so falsely proclaimed in many of our churches, where they recreate alleged "Biblical" truth, into their desired truth. They tend to do this, because the real truth is not always agreeable with their desired preferences, for the God they want to create in their minds, who "they" want God to be. Regardless of their desired God, this is often not the God of the Bible. Let's continue to think this through.

Over the years I wrestle with how a compassionate and loving God could have a Hell? Most Christians do. Inconceivable I thought! An eternal Hell is unthinkable even to consider. But there are other issues that I have struggled with at times, like the lasting and/or temporal benefits of being a good person. Some of the most prosperous people in this life are those who do not always play by the rules. Being good does not always appear to be pragmatically beneficial. Understanding that life is so short, we may come to ask ourselves at times, why limit our temporal life with restrictions that limit my pleasures or desired goals. There are two primary views. The one with our feet anchored in mid air, where truth is defined by personal preference, and the other, where truth and morality are anchored, in the very nature of God. These perspectives have significant ramifications, and they extend beyond today, into eternity. Where each viewpoint has significant eternal ramifications. And they all are related to what is actually true. And what is absolutely true, can only be anchored in the intrinsic nature of God.

This does not mean I like the repercussions of certain truths! However, my grappling with these eternal verities, eventually lead to a greater appreciation of the magnitude of God's immutable holy nature. While the consequences of Hell for the unredeemed are undeniably hard to accept, they are consistent with the infinite nature of God, and the lodgical ramifications of being immutably righteous. Disliking the consequences of a truth is not the same as the necessary inevitable results of it being true. The fact that remains is the standard of absolute holiness is inherent in the very nature of God, i.e. His immutable holiness. By growing in our comprehension of the immutable nature of God, we learn what He does is ultimately according to His nature, and therefore, just and fair for all of eternity. They are not usually according to our personal preference. Therefore, what we personally believe should never be the standard, unless it is anchored in truth.

My encouragement for the unbeliever, is to continue to pursue this study, in order to have a clear understanding of who God is in His very essence. And then to understand why that matters. The unbeliever needs to see the implications of God's holiness, which should result in their understanding of their need for deliverance, from the inevitable consequences of their sin. The necessary righteous judgment of sin. The upholding of the absolute righteousness standard that is inherent in the very nature of God. We all need a Savior! This is one of the principle reasons God has revealed Himself, so we know who He is in His personal essence. That standard is revealed, inpart, so we understand our predicament, and hopefully will pursue a salvific solution. We all need revealed and anchored truth. A universal standard that is not subject to every whim and personal preference.

For the believer, it is hopeful that this truth we are exploring, will motivate us to share with confidence, the hope we have in Christ. To be gospel oriented as ambassadors of Christ. It will further motivate us to be authentic in worship. To move past the superficial and often meaningless routine of our Christian walk, into eternally purposeful living. It will show that every detail of our lives matters to God, both now, and with the results of how we are living, manifesting in eternity. This is why a clear understanding of God's nature opens up the understanding of the gospel. These implications will be developed as we continue in the upcoming chapters.

(My reflections) I wanted to share with you that some of my struggles with these revelations were difficult to accept. My personal feeling was that I might be happier if I just abandon the practice of the faith. A freeing thought! Many believers have become so disillusioned with the hard realities of the faith that they have walked away. That may resolve the existential struggle, but the end result is we lose our hope. Because our hope is tied to the assurance that our faith is true. That God made promises that can be trusted because of his character. Also, it does not resolve the issues that are troubling us, there is still death, injustice and pain. Whether there is Hell or not, does not depend on my feelings about the subject. To think that there would never be final justice, or settled fairness, does not give any peace either. Reminding me that even without my Christain worldview, life can be very unfair. There was very little that would change if I did decide to walk away. It would only put my life on a path that would truly make my existence inconsequential. A temporary pursuit to avoid discomfort and find pleasure, but nothing eternal to hope for.

These reflections are part of the mental process I have labored to work through. The more I reflected on the intrinsic nature of God, the greater my insight into the implications of those attributes. In particular, the aspect of God's nature that stood out to me, was the absolutely holy nature of God, who is immutable. That set the standard. That defined the issue. Which led, naturally, to the reassuring hope we have in the gospel of Jesus Christ. But that conclusion came later in the resolution stage of my thinking. I still believe thinking through the process of deductive reasoning is beneficial. To suggest a conclusion, without the logical progressive reasoning, short changes some of the benefits of arriving at this understanding. The conclusions remain the same in the end, but we should still walk down this path of reasoning, through the implications to our conclusion, or we will need to go back and fill in the gaps in our thinking. Therefore, I think there is benefit to the chronological process of thinking this through, even though I am clearly Christian in my outcome. Now therefore, establishing the basis of truth, let us return to the deductive process, the resolving the who's God step. Because only the real God is the basis for ultimate truth.

CHAPTER 6

The confusion of who's God

I have often seen the bumper stickers on the back of vehicles that show numerous icons of the various major religious faiths. Oftentimes the symbols spell COEXIST, or a form of that, with the symbols of major religions spelling the word. There is this implied suggestion by this icon that all religions are equally true. The choice of which one to follow is a matter of personal preference. It is further implied by the message being portrayed, that we need to be accepting of others beliefs, and non-judgemental of their merits. That it is irreverent to these other faith traditions to claim one's own beliefs are true, and another belief tradition is false. It may even be suggested by some that advocating for one particular faith as true, over others, is a form of intolerance, thereby, offensive to those who hold to those alternative beliefs. The emphasis being portrayed is that all beliefs hold equal merit and we ought to "COEXIST" without judgment. But these fallacious perspectives deny any hope of arriving at absolute truth, since they have digressed to preferred truth.

Therefore, to assert my belief that the Christian faith is entirely true, logically indicates that the other traditions are not, or are lacking the whole truth. However, is that not inferred by those of other faith traditions, with their professed beliefs? By identifying with any belief traditions, they are in essence saying what they believe is true. It is illogical to practice a set of beliefs, if one does not believe what they profess to believe.

There are a number of reasons why people hold to a set of particular beliefs. It may simply be unexamined customs or beliefs that are familiar to their culture, and thereby passed on traditions. They are simply accepted because it was what they were taught. Or, for those not raised in a particular faith tradition, a belief that all faiths have personal merit, but their perspective satisfies an emotional or spiritual need in their life. One, that extends some sense of meaning of significance, beyond their existential struggles in an otherwise meaningless world. Lastly, for those who have abandoned the Christian faith, it may be the emotional distress, and unacceptability, of some of the harder truths inherent in Christianity. Which leads them to abandon the fundamentals of the Christian faith, and adopt another set of beliefs that are more harmonious with their preferred sense of fairness. Those who have left the faith for a more acceptable perspective of Christianity, may simply be unwilling to accept the notion of Hell, as an example. This is often described as progressive Christianity. A form of Christianity that denies some of the undesirable core beliefs and promotes universal equality.

This does not mean that there are no intellectual and emotional struggles with the Christian faith. There are, but that does not mean the Christian faith is not absolutely true. We need to think through those alleged problems to resolve these contentions. I realize there are numerous reasons people become disillusioned with the Christian faith. I am sure we all have felt this at some point in our Christian walk. It may be unanswered prayer, or the loss of a loved one, which leads to the feeling that God who is reportedly good, is not dependable in our time of need. These are a few of the emotional struggles we all share with the faith. Nevertheless, these enigmatic struggles are not always truth struggles. While these are true enigmas, the means for coming to a dependable faith requires one to assess the merits of our core beliefs, by answering the question of whether it is evidentiary true. This is one of the deficiencies of not thoroughly examining the abundance of evidence for the Christian faith. Once we establish the truthfulness of the faith, we are then better equipped to resolve some of those enigmas. This is part of the reason for this book. We are examining why God must act, as He does, in light of who He is.

Notwithstanding these struggles, there are considerable difficulties with this contention that all religions are generally equal. The first obstacle to overcome, it is impossible to reconcile the alleged truths of the various faiths, one faith with another. Therefore, it is transparent that all can be less than fully true, but they all cannot be entirely true. One's religious truth claims cannot be completely true, and any of the other faith claims be completely true at the same time, since they teach contrary beliefs. A truth claim cannot be true and not true at the same time. They simply do not hold to the same essential core beliefs. This is called the law of non-contradiction. I know of the moral fall of Ravi Zacharius, but he did a really nice job of explaining this principle. Many other Christian thinkers also make compelling arguments on why the differences between different faith traditions can not harmonize, one with another. It cannot be done when their core beliefs are in disagreement.

These various assertions of truth are relevant for us Christians to consider because we too make truth claims. Take for example, the Gospel of John, chapter 14 verse 6. In the New International Version, it reads; Jesus answered, "I am the way and the truth and the life. No one comes to the Father except through Me." As Dr. Andy Woods has noted in one of his sermons, take note of the definite article, "the". He is "the" way, He is "the" truth, He is "the" life. Jesus does not say He is "a" way. So while all religions can have aspects of truth in what they teach, they all cannot be absolutely true, since, once again, they contradict each other! So our question is; did Jesus tell the truth? If He did, then all other faith traditions are in their essence, less than absolute truth. Simply because, what Jesus said, is quantitatively different from all other faith traditions. What He claims is; He is "the" only way. He is "the" truth. His truth claims are simply irreconcilable with the claims of the other faith traditions. Either He is telling the truth or He is not! These are not just personal preferences. What we believe has eternal significance. What we accept as true determines our eternal destiny. Not only does He claim to be "the" truth, He claims, He is the only way to the Father! He uses exclusive claims, like "no one" and "except through Me", as the way to God the Father. It is a claim to be the exclusive path to God the Father. It has eternal repercussions in the very claims of stated truth. (Read again John 14:6)

Of course, we need to show Christian love in all circumstances, but that does not mean that we accept every belief as valid. Truth is truth regardless of our individual desires. This is also why we Christians need to be cautious with those who claim to have visions or revelations from God. A major world religion and the Mormans both started with an alleged vision from an Angel. But remember, Satan too masquerades as an angel of light. There are some litmus tests for us who are believers, who hold to the truthfulness of Christianity. Consider, as an example, the claims of the deity of Christ, and the sufficiency of His death on the cross, which is the basis for salvation. Both are absolutely crucial to be considered a born again Christain. The complete authority of the scriptures is high on that list too. But ultimately, it comes down to, who is Jesus Christ? A great teacher of moral principles or Almighty God in flesh? Our only trustworthy redeemer?

These truth claims should also determine the reason we fellowship as a body of believers. The unifying aspect of joining a local Christian church is that we agree with the nature of God, the doctrine, and mission given to the church. At least it should be! It should be more than the preference of music and likability of the people, or even the charisma of the pastor. The unity around those core beliefs should determine the reason we gather as a body of believers. Therefore, a denial of those core tenets of Christianity, and the exclusive message of John 14:6, has enormous ramifications. When we abandon these core Biblical truths, we lose the very reason for existing as a body of believers. We were called to be the beacon of light in a dark world. That light grows dim when we depart from truth, or when we join the chorus of religious voices that are void of trustworthy eternal truths. When this takes place, we as the body of Christ, lose the very reason for existing. We would have no message of eternal worth. No real truth to proclaim. We become nothing more than a subset of culture. A group of individuals, who share together what they desire to be true, but not the actual truth.

When the truth of what we believe is abandoned, waterdown or neglected, we have lost the reason for the gospel. How do we value the work of Christ on the cross, if we do not grasp the immutable holiness of God? If we lose our understanding of the absolute holiness of God, we lose our motivation for sharing our faith. Why share the gospel if there is no need? The precious hope contained in the gospel message is compromised when we deny Hell.

Even when churches desire to maintain a quasi evangelical presence, so they can retain the claim to be an evangelical church, the abandonment of core truth often leads to erroneous gospel presentations. I have listened to sermons advocating the need for the unbeliever to be saved. (A salvation message) Only to have the pastor mistaken on the core elements of Christianity. There are fundamental truths that are necessary to know, and believe, to become a Christian. How does one appropriate the merits of what Christ did on the cross when the salvation message is vague and confusing? The merits of Christ's sacrifice are magnified when the mind is opened to essential core truths of the Christian faith. These are tied together into inseparable truths. And when these are not held together, we lose the gospel to confusion. And this all starts with whose God are we following. A message has no chance of being salvific, if we start on the wrong track, with the wrong God. But even when we are on the right track, with the right God, many distort the clarity of the gospel. A few examples to show what I mean.

Often the gospel is presented as asking Jesus into one's heart. What does it mean to ask Jesus into one's heart? Where even is that verse in the Bible? It is a confusing and unbiblical message! (See Pastor Dennis Rokser's book on this subject from Grace Gospel Press) Or, making a commitment to Christ to become a Christian. The first question should be how much of a commitment is sufficient? This is needed information to have assurance of salvation. This unqualified and subjective standard would be troublesome for me. Anyone who truly assesses their own life in light of God's immutable holiness could never have peace that they are saved. How do you qualify a human commitment with the infinite? When is it enough? Remember when Christ called His disciples to abandon everything and follow Him, not to even look back. If absolute commitment, as called forth by Christ, is a condition for salvation, I have never met a true Christian! To compound the problem with requiring a commitment for salvation, there is not one verse that calls an unbeliever to make a commitment to be saved. There are many verses that call for believers to make a commitment to fervent discipleship. To become mature saints we need to be diligent in our discipleship. Stay with me, as I will address these subjects as we progress in the book.

These subjects are immensely important to this whole conversation. When we fall into error in our teachings, or even who is God, we lose the very message of our Christian salvation. We also need to be cautious that we don't invoke the warnings of the Apostle Paul as recorded in his letter to the Galatians. Adding or distracting anything to the gospel message has eternal consequences. That is why knowing God's attributes are absolutely essential. This is not just how to live out a quality subjective Christian faith.

Since, everything we profess to believe, is based on who, and what is, "the" truth. As illustrated, impart, in the marriage example. Therefore, the truth about which God we are worshiping, and the attributes of God's distinct holiness, need to be magnified, for there to be a clear Biblical gospel salvation message. For without this Biblical accurate message of salvation truth, we are left with a confusing message. Our eyes are still blinded to salvation essentials. We are then no longer able to present the all-important teachings of the faith. The end result is, we lose our message and our reason for sharing the message, the only trustworthy message that gives eternal confidence. Is this not what we are seeing? I will address the essential salvation details later in the book.

(My editorial) It is my allegation that the American Church has neglected a comprehensive pursuit of the knowledge of the nature of God. There are aspects of God's nature that are crucial if we want to be theologically sound Christians. Unfortunately, pulpits are often silent on these essential truths that make Christianity, authentic Christianity. What greater knowledge can there be for the Christian, but to know who is the real God, and what is His very immutable essence. Everything related to our practice and mission is dependent on this understanding. A faulty understanding of who God is, or even a deficiency of understanding, and everything we hold true, is subject to either confusion, or a misunderstanding of the very faith we profess. Should that be the case, then how we live, our purpose as a body of believers, and our message will be diminished. Or worse, even useless. The first area to be compromised is likely going to be the failure to grasp the truth of exclusivity of who Christ is, and what He did. (John 14:6) If we don't understand the pending consequences the non-believer is going to encounter upon death, we will have nothing to offer as the ultimate hope. Or, even more subtle, is finding ourselves proclaiming a useless, non Biblical salvation message. To avoid this, all starts by ensuring that we have the right understanding of who God is. No other alleged religion besides Biblical Christianity has these credentials, nor an accurate understanding of who is "the" truth. An exclusive claim from the very mouth of our Lord Jesus Christ. I address salvation principles more in chapters 8, 9, 10 and 11.

1. Sermon by Dr. Andy Woods @SLBC Andy Woods Sermon on the Gospel of John 14:5-7

CHAPTER 7

Looking at the values in a life without God

I briefly want to look at one more fundamental reason why we need to make sure we are on the right path, before we move on into the meat of this book. I do not intend on spending a significant amount of time on this subject. There are countless books on how to live a life that is meaningful, and one that is ultimately purposeful. It would be like chasing a rabbit, Zig and zagging, without getting anywhere relevant. And a pursuit of that nature would take us beyond the intent of this book. Although, how we live as Christians, is one of the primary emphasis of the book. Therefore, I want to address a few additional points that relate to living eternally relevant lives. For those who desire to live a life that has an enduring impact, a few additional thoughts might be helpful.

If one returns their thoughts to the marriage illustration in chapter four of this book. We see the implications of living a morally relevant life in light of God's holy design for marriage. Marriage is defined by God as an intended sacred union, solely for a man and women. A union that only makes sense when understood in this light. Outside of this God given purpose, the marriage union could be seen as little more than a sexually limiting arrrangment. Your view of marriage, as a sacred union, depends on the premise of one's morality. This again returns to what is the foundation for morals. Which we Christians should answer, is the inherent nature of God, Himself. So to those who do not hold our perspective, we may ask it in the form of a question; why be moral? A simple, but far reaching question. Which can be answered in different shades, according to the distinct implications of how the question is being posed, and morals held.

As an example, one can argue for the enumerable sociological reasons, and there are many. It is clear that the stability of society is strengthened by traditional marriage. Children do much better in every aspect of life, in a loving, supportive, and Biblically based stable home. That each, a man and women, bring attributes of their own that benefit the development of an emotionally strong child. Particularly, when each member is manifesting those qualities, that emanate from being solidly grounded in the faith. Therefore, even outside the Biblical mandate, society has valid reasons to support the stability of traditional marriages. It is the optimal way to live for both a healthy society, and the emotional wellbeing of children, which is dependent for a large part on the stability and quality of their parents' marriage. Even later as adults, the dependability of their parents' marriage continues to give stability to their lives. It is God's plan. Which always works best.

The alternative is also true, if there is no God to ultimately answer to, why is marriage an exclusive relationship that needs to be honored? Why object to the previous illustrated marriage arrangement in chapter 4? If I am going to live a short meaningless life, and then die! Therefore, these evaluations of our morality are all dependent on what God has said. And what He has said in the scriptures is a reflection of His innate nature. As I previously argued in the illustration, there are no coherent moral violations in the marriage illustration, if there is no immutable and holy God. The logic is solid. The man and women both, it can be argued, have benefits from the agreed extra marital relationship. She has the freedom to explore her sexual urges, to pursue her lustful desires. He has benefited from a more expressive sexual encounter. No other negative implications can be logically alleged if the holiness of God is removed from the equation. The potential consequences are those that relate to jealousy of the partner, and the ethical nature of the relationship. However, where do these morals derive from? Why don't we all pursue this arrangement as illustrated? Seriously, sex is enjoyable! Why not explore sex to the maxium? In light of the temporary nature of life this seems reasonable and logical. That should be the logical conclusion of those who reject the moral teachings of the scriptures. I still would not suggest that course of action, because the results are never good, but there is logic to the thinking. The question always returns to; what has God said? And why has this been revealed in the scriptures as the only pattern for marriage? It can be simply stated, it is because it is who He is in His consument righteousness. Therefore, a reflection of Him, and the best way to live long and healthy, and stable lives. Otherwise, there is no anchor on which to base our morality. It is leaving this foundation that has rippled through our society, particularly, when we lose this foundational perspective. These reasonsoning are called "Reductio Ad Absurdum". Ideas that are taken to their logical conclusions show how absolutely absurd they really are.

This is the temptation that many face as they age. They see this life as passing by and reach for fleeting satisfaction. They feel the burdens of life and want to escape from the mundane aspects of life. They want to recapture the erotic illutions of youth, only to realize that it caused irrevocable regret and pain. What looks like renewed freedom only results in remorse and regret. And most often results in a broken relationship. This too is destructive to the lives of those around them. We do not live on islands. Every choice has ripple effects. Do you really want another man or woman raising your kids while you are still paying for their keep? Raising them or disciplining them in a manner that you would disapprove of, and holding to different values than we desire to impress upon them. Or, if you are in a later stage of life, do you want to give up half of everything you have labored for all your life? In either situation, there are issues regarding holidays and special family events. We find ourselves sharing holidays with those that are not our own, while our own children spend those times with unrelated relatives of the parent's new spouse. Or, sadly, one is left trying to celebrate those major events alone. This is why leaving the foundations of Biblical faith leads to so many unintended negative consequences.

In addition to those potential consequences. Why do we resist these impulses? Is it simply because of expective societal norms? It may even be argued that for society it is better to be moral and hold to the sacredness of marriage, but not in my individual interest. Again, in light of the temporary nature of life, this may seem rational and logical. Why subject my egocentric sexual interest for the benefit of society? Considering there is no moral underpinnings to consider this wrong, that is, without God. Is it simply our culture passing on expectation that limit my sexual experiences.

A few contrasting thoughts on the implications of marriage in light of knowing the nature of God. There is a divine plan for mankind. The practical aspects of life are affected regardless if one is a believer or not. God's plan just works better for all.

The further we drift from Biblical morality the more acceptable this perverse idea becomes. The decision of whether to adhere to the fidelity to marriage becomes one of current culture norms, and not a moral expectation established by God, as John Stonestreet has expounded on, in a Colson Center Podcast. He remarked that marriage was previously more like gravity, meaning an absolute. Now society treats marriage as a speed limit, subject to the changing values of culture. What was once a traditional stabilizing belief, has now has become a fading Christian standard. This is because we have adopted those emerging values as our culture changes.

As noted, it is interesting that even those outside the normal Christian identity, in general, hold to the expectation that marriage is to be exclusive and a faithful standard between two people. But why? This is a functioning relationship in the illustration. What is there to object to? That is, if both parties agree with this arrangement. For that matter, what harm is there if these activities occurred, and no knowledge was discovered? It is the knowledge of the actions that causes the emotional pain for the one betrayed. The unsuspecting spouse is not emotionally harmed if they are unaware of others activities.

However, for the Christian, God knows, and He holds the marriage bed as sacred. And He will hold us accountable either in this life, or at the Bema Seat judgment, or both. (Both of these consequences will be discussed later) Let alone the practical consequences of being caught, the guilt and the hurt inflicted by the betrayal. The betrayal discovered has lasting consequences, forever altering the basis of trust. Which alters God's plan for the family. Solid, Godly, and lasting marriage is clearly the desired plan of God. It promotes the stability of society. It allows us to sleep at night, knowing we are living according to the revealed standards of our Heavenly Father. God has equipped us with a conscience. Guilt is difficult to live with. One of many aspects of the Holy Spirit's ministry is the conviction of sin. What the world too often accepts, will always clearly be considered gravity for us Bible believers. Over the last hundred years as the church and society have drifted from Biblical truth, the more prevalent and acceptable these choices have become. This is evident with the removal of Bible reading and prayer in school in the early 60's. Take some time and study the results to our country when we abandoned those foundations. The explosion of the sexual revolution. The resulting consequences to our nation, and to us, individually. It has been detrimental to our quality of life.

Regardless of the changing values of society, God's immutable standards do not change. This is why we need to renew our minds, so when we start to meander in thought and entertain lustful thoughts, we remember that there are consequences to choices. We quickly count the cost. What society may now find acceptable, will always be a Biblical principle from our Heavenly Father. Those principles reveal His nature. He will not alter His opinion just because society has.

I certainly believe in God's forgiveness, and I believe He can rebuild broken lives, but it was never His desired plan. In the beginning, God created man and woman to become one flesh. God has done amazing things in many fractured relationships, but the pain should have been avoided. That is why God has spoken. His way is always the better way. It is the only way to eternal life, and the best way to live an eternally significant life, a meaningful life.

It is not always easy, those commitments we make in life, but we sacrificed. My wife stayed home with the kids when they were young. I am not saying it was the only way, but I never regretted giving up some material things to have my wife home. She loves being a mom. It gave stability to the home. It was a chapter in our lives. Later my wife went back to college and became a RN. Finding fulfillment in a career. But there were priorities we held as of greater importance. Our focus was to invest in raising our children. It took a lot of hard work. I believe we did a reasonably good job. This is evident on the fact that they are not dependent on us for their daily subsistence. That's also the hard part of letting go at the end of the process. You are successful in part, if you are not depended upon for daily substance. They are self-sufficient and are managing life well as adults, passing on many of the values that were taught as youths.

It is losing the daily interaction with them we enjoyed while they were living at home that is hard to let go of. It is the natural part of life. They move on in their journey of life. Thankfully, we continue to maintain a good relationship with them, but like chapters in a book, that one has passed. They are now focused on their responsibilities of parenthood and life. It is the way it should be. I told them when they started having families of their own, that every emotion they would ever have, will be magnified when they have children of their own. This is the journey of life. The foundation is the home and the values that are taught there. The other perspective results in detrimental natural consequences that result from deviating from the inherent foundational values of the Christian faith. There is a practical absurdity of abandoning those Christian values. See what despair we are creating by leaving the foundations of the Biblical faith.

Hopefully, one can see the logic of my argument. I believe the absurdity of the marriage illustration is clear. We all naturally hold values. Those values established by God, and violated, have consequences. A meaningful life is a purposeful life that is lived with God's perspective in view. I am going to leave this subject a bit unfinished. (Not sure even if it was a chapter worth leaving in the book. However, a few reinforcing reflections, might be helpful for some, so I left it in) I will argue as the book progresses the reasons why we individually, as a body of believers, and as a society, should understand these subjects in light of God's unchangeable holiness. The most significant is our need to be brought into a right relationship with God. There is simply no subject more important than where we will spend eternity. These questions are addressed in the next four chapters.

CHAPTER 8

Let's explore the perfect immutably of God's nature

Accepting my original assumptions that God exists and the Bible portrays the only reliable description of His nature, let's continue the thought process. We all know this present physical journey of life has built in limitations. There is an unavoidable day when each member of the human race enters eternity. Therefore, there is an unmistakable importances of knowing God's requirements. What will He require of me to be with Him? To help in this understanding, it is crucial that we have some understanding of the standards of God. We need to know what determines those standards. For this to be understood, we need to know God's attributes. We need some theological descriptions of those attributes. I have eluded to them a number of times. I now need to give greater clarity to these attributes. Not only do these need to be understood, these need to be kept in the forefront of your minds throughout the reading of this book. My presumptive arguments for this book are dependent on these truths. These are my lay interpretations, not scholarly, but I believe them to be accurate just the same.

The first is holiness, the only attribute of God that is used in the Bible, trifold. The use of this description of God, is in the books of Revelation and Isaiah. It is the descriptive emphasis of God's unique and total separation from anything sinful. And, therefore, it may be argued that it is the most essential attribute, since it is the only described attribute of God that is used trifold. Holy is simply what we would commonly understand by the term. While God is by nature loving, it may be said that His holiness is central to who He is, because of the usage in those two books.

When man is exposed to God manifesting this revelation of His nature, it results in praise, relevant fear, the awe, worship and adoration of God's being. It is being taken back by the fact that God is; Holy, Holy, Holy. Here are three practical examples, as exemplified in the Bible.

First, I am thinking of 1 Chronicles, chapter 13. The Israelites were moving the Ark of God and it became unsteady. Uzzah placed his hand on the Ark to steady it, and was instantly killed. He touched the holiness of God's Glory. Even though it may have appeared his actions were noble, God's holiness cannot be compromised, or infringed upon.

Second, would be the requirements for entering the most holy place of the temple. Where only the High Priest would enter to meet with God once a year. Thereby, indicating that this was not something to take haphazardly, or presumptuously. That entering God's presence was sacred, and needed to be done with utmost respect, and in a very prescribed manner.

Thirdly, in the description by Jesus of John the Baptist, whom He called the greatest of all prophets. Yet, John, understanding the holiness of Jesus, declared he was unworthy to even untie Jesus' dirty sandals. (Mark 1:7) Think for a moment about that contrast. The greatest of all prophets was unworthy to untie the dirty sandals of the Lord Jesus Christ. There are countless more. Complete books would not be enough to explore this profound attribute.

But ultimately, the best description of the nature of God, is that He lives in unapproachable light. Think about this for a moment before moving on. Living in unapproachable light. (1Timothy 6:16) And, in reflection, certainly what we honestly lack. It is ludicrous to think that in any aspect I could consider myself holy. If we believe we are holy or righteous, in the absolute sense, it indicates a very faulty and fundamental misunderstanding of the absolute holiness of God. This is also the standard by which He will one day judge us. He Himself is the standard. Since the standard is God Himself, to be in His presence, requires a standing of absolute holiness. Most every aspect of life has a system, or means to measure, to see if something measures up to a standard. God Himself is the standard. Unmitigated holiness is inherent in His very nature. Let's be clear here, you do not measure up!

The second, would be that He is intrinsically holy in His nature. Webster defines intrinsic as belonging to the essential nature or constitution of a thing. What something is in its very essence. God is who God is! He is perfect in every and all aspects. He has a nature that is absolutely holy, and the nature God possesses, is incomparably holy to any other being. God in His essence is in a class by Himself that has no comparison. In the Old Testament, He simply describes Himself, as I Am who I Am. The mild difference may be described as; holiness is an attribute possessed as God, and that attribute is the intrinsic nature of who He is as God. It is inseparable from who He is! Think of this way, I may have attributes, but that does not mean I have them intrinsically in myself, as God does. I have been given this created nature by God, but He has that nature intrinsically.

Thirdly, and just as essential, God is love. It is another aspect of His intrinsic nature. Love originates in the very nature of God. Therefore, as the origin of love, God is a loving and compassionate God. It is an aspect of being the triune God. His nature is just that; loving kindness. This attribute is portrayed in His long-suffering kindness, which is expressed repeatedly throughout the scriptures. As the source of love, the greatest expression of love, is the cross of Christ. He is not wanting anyone to perish, but all to come to repentance (change their mind), and accepting the gift He is offering. This gift, that is the being offered, is the gift of eternal salvation, and forgiveness of sin. Which is made possible because the Lord Jesus Christ, Himself, paid our sin debt on the cross. Which upon personal acceptance by a believing sinner, results in our eternal salvation. (As we will explore in more detail in the coming chapters)

Fourly, is the understanding that He is immutable. This is the idea that God cannot change. Not only is His nature intrinsically holy, it is an unchangeable righteous nature. He will never get better, nor decline in that attribute. He is by nature, is who He is, and to change would cause Him to be less than the incomparable, immutable, and intrinsically holy God, as described in the Bible. This is an eternal state. He will never ever be other than what He is, or ever can be, eternal and immutability, holy! This is one that really grabbed my attention over the last few years. An immutable holy God. And this understanding is absolutely essential if we want to truly grasp the significance of the gospel. He cannot compromise His nature, and it will never ever change!

Next, for the purpose of this descriptive focus, He is omnipotent. The description starts in the very beginning, in the book of Genesis. From the very beginning, God created. The creative, and majestic power of God, can be seen in the act of creating the whole universe simply by His command. It is unfathomable to grasp the power that God possesses. He has the power to do whatever He desires as long as it does not conflict with His nature. This is significant for us to understand. While it may at first appear to be an unsolvable tension, it does have a divine solution. There is a means for which God can be simultaneously, both immutable holy and immutably loving, without ever compromising either essential attribute.

Lastly, to help in the foundational understanding of what I am attempting to communicate in this book, is that God is omniscience. He will never learn anything. He knows everything and is indefectible in that knowledge. Not only is His nature immutable and holy, He also possesses absolute knowledge of everything. I am always learning and relearning, not so with God. God knows both actual and potentially, everything. The idea that God does not know every aspect of my life, both potentially and/or actually, misunderstands omniscience. This means every thought too. To think that someday, I will stand before this Almighty God, and have any hope that He will not be totally mindful of my behavior, or can overlook any of my sinful actions, is wishful thinking. It is certainly not a Biblical truth. Think about that the next time you entertain a thought or engage in an action that is not consistent with who we are called to be as Christians. Alternatively, if you have not come to benefit from the person and work of Jesus Christ on the cross, this knowledge of your behavior is still subject to the absolute standard, He Himself. This idea that God does not remember every minute detail about our lives is not a Biblical truth. He does, and the standard for judgment is still the same, His immutable holy nature!

The Gospel will never be fully understood and appreciated, or accurately presented, until these concepts are clear in the mind of believers, and to a lesser degree, unbelievers. Since unbelievers need to understand their need for salvation, before they can understand the redeeming work of the God/man, the only Savior, Jesus Christ. Therefore, it is of the utmost importance that these truths are understood, and repeatedly emphasized.

He is holy, that is His intrinsic nature, and it cannot change, ever! He is the unchangeable and incomparable holy God. A bit redundant, but necessary to get these points established. These concepts are the principle building blocks for everything I want to address in this book, particularly, for the next few chapters.

1. The difficulty using particular references for these chapters is that this information has been found in dozens and dozens of books that I have read. I used a generalization of all that material. Please check out the Bibliography. In general they all address the same salvation themes.

CHAPTER 9

A dilemma

There is only so much we can know just by observation of the world. It is easy to see God's creative power, just open your eyes. Stare at the sky on a clear night. Look through a telescope. But most other aspects of God's nature need to be understood by revelation. Since if He did not reveal, we could only speculate on His nature. Thankfully, He did in the pages of the scriptures. Our only trustworthy source for knowing the Creator, our Heavenly Father. There are essential attributes of His nature that simply could not be known without that divine revelation. For example, we would not know He is holy. We could look at the injustices of this world, and surmise that God is extremely powerful, but imperfect in moral character, if nature and humanity are a reflection of His nature. We may see unanswered injustice, and not know that He is the ultimate source of justice. That in eternity, every wrong will be made right, and perfect justice will be administered. The more we understand science, the better we understand His unfathomable intelligence, this through scientific discovery, and by exploring the intricate design of the universe. These discoveries help us to grasp a bit of the beyond this world wisdom in creation. When we experience suffering, we might not recognize He is the source of compassion, which is sometimes hard to perceive in light of the fallenness of this world. Therefore, we may not always comprehend that He, in His essential nature, is a loving and compassionate God. We may see glimpses of His loving kindness, hopefully expressed by His children, but the full assurance of His loving kindness does not come, until we are confident that eventually He will wipe every tear away, and restore His creation in perfect righteousness. This becomes even more comforting when we understand He has a plan, for the renewed perfection of His creation, in the coming Eternal Kingdom. (Revelation chapter 21)

Thankfully, God chose to reveal Himself for our benefit, for without that revelation we would not understand the dilemma that we started to explore in the last chapter. Always keeping in mind, He has revealed clearly that He is holy, but is also a compassionate and loving God. Which is encouraging to know in this very harsh world in which we live. However, when we start this journey, our first impression of the revelation of His absolute holiness, as described, is likely dread, maybe even outright fear. This should be the naturally expected reaction of knowing that we in ourselves do not meet this standard. Yet, this is the necessary first step in understanding our need. It is almost like pain. Pain is what often drives us to the doctor, whereby we are diagnosed, and get needed treatment. If we did not know our need, we likely would not seek a solution. We needed to know our utter sinfulness before the justice seat of a holy God, before we would seek deliverance from a qualified Savior, otherwise, we would die in ignorance. Can you imagine dying in an unsaved state, and meeting God, and for the first time you understand His nature and yours, a problem discovered too late.

Let's start with some more introductory thoughts, a preview and review of this situation, because of the eternal significance. Without this basic knowledge, most people are depending on their own perceived goodness, which is a faulty standard to gauge one's qualifications for heaven. This is why these chapters are so extremely important. Because when we fail to grasp this essential understanding of unmitigated holiness, that is inherent in God, we are oblivious to the problem. His unapproachable holiness, which is the standard, that God must uphold to be true to Himself. Consequently, without this knowledge, unbelievers have no understanding of the required status needed to be in God's presence. Then when the event happens, as it will for all of us, that someone steps over the line of death, and finds irrevocable horror, it is then simply too late. The consequences are irreversible and forever. Trying to help think this through with some preliminary thoughts, even if it is repeatedly discussed, it is just that important! So let's continue our exploration of this subject, and move forward, even if it is a bit redundant to some.

I want to go over this one more time, because we need this diagnosis of our problem, for us to understand the necessary solution. This is really indispensable information. There are innumerable individuals, who will pontificate on their understanding of what is necessary to meet God's standards. Their surmising about the qualifications for entrance into this final state. How they hope to qualify for heaven. Oftentimes they can be even a bit confident. Surmising that they in themselves are deserving of heaven, but it is just speculation on their part. They don't have a valid reference point to gauge qualifications for acceptance. Their gauge of goodness or acceptable righteousness, is their self-comparison to the culture around them. They surmise that they are better than most. They point to some good qualities in their life as evidence for this opinion. However, this is a faulty grasp of true divine holiness, society standards were never the standard with God, His nature is! Those trusting in their own subjective goodness have not come to understand God's perspective of holiness. Unfortunately, most don't even pursue this understanding. They will spend more time planning a vacation or retirement, than inquiring about what God says about the subject. One can be a relatively good person but not holy. Not in the absolute sense. I know many good people. I never met one absolutely holy. The standard is the intrinsic and immutable holiness that is the essence of God's nature, and that is what God will require. Perfection! I am sorry to tell you, holiness is not inherent in you! You need it to be granted to you from another source, because it is unattainable to be achieved on your own.

Let's pause and remember the undeniable truth about life. We will all eventually enter the next stage of life, the eternal. It is coming. No stopping it. Death is as sure as anything we will ever experience in this life. And the matter is generally ignored for the pursuit of personal, but temporal fulfillment, even in our churches. We are okay with general goodness. We just feel extremely uncomfortable with preaching on required holiness. But what God demands to be in His presence is absolute perfection. When we first come to this knowledge, it is like, oh crap, I have an enormous problem. A huge and apparently unsolvable one. At least one we have the ability to solve on our own.

May I step back and reflect for a moment. Truthfully, at times, I wish there was a different way. A general goodness that was acceptable. I had once thought the removal of these perfect standards would be easier to mentally live with. The basic goodness that we generally find in most of mankind. I desired to set aside the thoughts of absolutes for salvation, and simply enjoy the goodness of life. I personally prefer relative morality. We all do! But if that were the case? How would we define that standard? At first it may appear to be a relief, that I may be able on my own, to achieve the standard God requires. However, when you start to ponder, how to gauge if one measures up, that would give little relief. We could never know for sure. What if I was wrong in my assessment? Thinking that I have merited this good standing, only to be wrong in the end, horribly wrong! In deeper reflection, I prefer the perfect standard, knowing that it is not I who is able to meet it, but Jesus Christ, and His sacrifice on the cross who does for me. Then I can have the confidence that is assured. An assurance that is dependable, and eternally trustworthy. Please allow me the chance to elaborate on those ideas as we continue. I just wanted to reflect for a moment.

Let's resume with the logic of the argument. I am left with this dilemma, I believe the Bible gives an accurate reflection of God's perfect standard. His standards are a reflection of His nature. Having come to this belief, which makes perfect sense, as I would expect nothing less from God. Who wants to worship an compromised and less than perfect God? Who would want to worship a sinful God? One that is flawed like us. There would be no ultimate basis for justice. Even the rapist would have a defense against God's justice. One could claim, you too are a sinner like me, so by what standard gives you a right to judge me? (Then again, how does one even define evil, if there is no intrinsic immutable holy God? A perfect standard that is inherent in a perfect person. Just reflecting, I do that alot. That is why I am writing a book) The clear teaching regarding God is that He is; Holy, Holy, Holy. There is simply no other way of understanding the revealed nature of God, other than He is who He is! He is, and always will be, immutably holy. Let's continue....

Coming to grips with this is difficult, but is logically expected, if one considers what a perfect God must be like. It is also the revealed truth by the Holy Spirit, and not able to be understood without this Biblical revelation. So whether by gentle persuasion, or terrifying truth encounter, this is the straightward truth about God. And that truth has eternal repercussions. (That again is why I am writing an evangelistic book)

I had thoughts of what it would be like to cross over to the other side (enter eternity) and become face to face with the infinitely holy God who knows everything about everything. He knows our thoughts and our actions and our motivations. And being rejected! Can you even ponder for a moment what it would be like to be irrevocably rejected. There will be no argument or defense. What can I argue before an all knowing God? He cannot change His standards. What a horrifying thought. Read about the rich man in the Gospel of Luke, chapter 16. The agony of His experience was actual and irrevocable. Interesting, he suddenly became interested in evangelism, which is a little late now! There is no more horrifying thought that could ever be considered by man, than being irrevocably lost for all of eternity. I don't like it. I hate the notion. How can this be? There is no way to soften this reality. Generally, why Christians and churches ignore this topic. It is hard to grapple with the implications. Who even wants to consider the possibility? We are often embarrassed to admit this is what we believe, so we quickly move on to a new subject, even though this is the premiere question of all time. While difficult to accept, its importance is undeniable.

This is why a better understanding of absolute holy is so crucial, for both the believer and the unbeliever. And why this needs to be clearly taught in our local churches. It is also why we individually need to accept the reality of God's distinctiveness, even though we may feel repulsed by the ramifications. It is who He is and we are not. It is the reality of the situation. I don't have a say in the matter. My preferred opinion does not matter, nor does what I want to believe matter, He cannot change who He is.

Furthermore, this understanding defines our missions as a body of believers. And should give pause to the unbeliever, to reconsider their implicit need for deliverance, from their precarious situation, how to escape the eternal consequences of their inevitable. Their lack of standing before the justice seat of God's absolute holiness. Until this is realized, there appears no reason to look for a potential solution. Why look for a solution, if there is no awareness of the coming consequences? This results because we lack an accurate knowledge of God's required standards. And when this understanding is lacking, we miss the central message of the Bible. It could be summarized in three steps of truth. The first is obvious, this life is temporal, and death is inevitable. The second two need divine revelation. The first of these second two; is the revelation that God is absolutely holy, and cannot alter His standards. Lastly, He loves us enough to create a complete solution to our inherent sin problem. Or, as I like to do, and ask in the form of a question; how can an immutable holy God have a relationship with an inherently sinful man? The answer magnifies a person, who is the Lord Jesus Christ, and His sacrifice on the cross. So we start by coming to an understanding of the nature of the problem. The dilemma! Let's continue to explore God's marvelous solution to this unavoidable predicament. What determines our place in eternity?

1. The difficulty using particular references for these chapters is that this information has been found in dozens and dozens of books that I have read. I used a generalization of all that material. Please check out the Bibliography. In general they all address the same salvation themes.

CHAPTER 10

The need and reasonableness of the Gospel

This comes back to my primary focus in this book. This is not a new profound revelation. Some grand insight that I just learned that nobody else has discovered. It is a simple return to what has been the historical understanding of God. I am simply drawing attention back to some foundational truths of the faith that have been forsaken for a variety of reasons. Both in the church and practically by most individual Christians. These next two chapters are likely the most significant chapters in my book. It is the one subject that has too often been ignored. How to find deliverance from the consequences of our sin. There is simply no greater need for mankind, than to know the need, and then, accept the means of salvation. The eternity of one's soul dependents on it. Knowing the problem is the first step. God is immutably holy! We are not! Let's continue with the progression of the thought process.

One would think that the obvious is so apparent that this would be the ultimate pursuit. The, I need to know, that I know for sure, where I will spend eternity. There is no question in life that should be of greater concern. What happens after death? Because the consequences are so final. The expected and assumed natural desire, should be, to know if there is an answer. A quest to know if God has designed a plan to solve our humanly unsolvable dilemma. I have already alluded to the answer in the previous chapters. It is now time to focus more intently into the resolution of our problem. The answer. Since it is clear we have no way to bridge the chasm between us. We are sinners by nature and deed. We do not have the means to resolve our hopeless situation, or change our sinful nature. If there is a solution, it is up to God, because we literally need a divine solution.

These are the questions. How does God set forth the restoring of this broken relationship? What was God's dilemma, when it comes to restoring His relationship with mankind? How could God express His love and not compromise His holiness? The proper understanding of His nature is undeniably, and essential, to understanding the problem. Actually, it was a solution God had in the timeless past, He just needed to reveal it, so we could have the opportunity to respond to it.

While mankind is the one who is facing the consequences of the sin problem, only God has the ability to solve it. After a perfect creation everything changed. Adam, the father of mankind, once in relationship and fellowship with God, became broken by willful sin. By sinning, he became a sinner, and passed that nature on to us. (I will clarify the difference between the two later, relationship and fellowship) The Apostle Paul deals with this ultimate issue in the book of Romans, chapter 3. There Paul writes about God needing to be just, and also the justifier. Notice that He does not change His standards. He is just. Another indicator of His holy nature and disposition, or state of consummate righteousness. He is just because by His nature it is who He is. A judge who does not administer justice, is not just. And in this case, absolutely and forever, perfect righteousness is the standard. A terrifying thought, no doubt. Please understand by repeating these themes, I am trying to anchor these truths in your minds! This is an eternally crucial truth!

Furthermore, the clear indication of that verse is only He is able to justify the sinner, since it is clear we cannot undo our sinful condition, nor reverse those we already committed. To further our predicament, not only can we not erase our sinful past, nor stop from sinning, we are unable to measure up to His never-ending perfect righteousness. Actually, we are in an humanly unresolvable situation, therefore, indicating only God can affect this change of status, that is needed in the life of the unbelieving sinner. We need God to be our justifier!

When I was teaching in my jail ministry, (before covid) I would use this illustration to demonstrate the contrast. This is the litmus test that will tell if we are understanding the predicament correctly? I would explain to those in my class using this contrast. That when one understands that God is so holy, that the most insignificant, the most trivial or benign sin, is enough to keep one from being in God's presence for all of eternity, then they are beginning to understand intrinsic holiness as it relates to God's nature. And His justice requires an atonement, an payment, as a consequence for violating His standard. His nature requires an uncompromising separation from the sin, since sin and holiness cannot coexist. And whatever unatoned sin exists, would remain forever, in an unforgiven state. Therefore, he who possesses that sin nature must be separated from the holiness of God.

However, and thankfully, the work of Christ is so complete, that the most vial, the most evil and/or disgusting sin, is fully atoned (paid for) by the sufficient work of Jesus Christ on the cross. That is the litmus test of both the holiness of God, and the sufficiency of the person (the God/man, Jesus Christ), and the indispensabile need for the payment of our sin by Him on the cross. It is crucial to understanding these twin truths, since it is the essence of what makes the Gospel so grand. Both the satisfaction of the required holiness of God, and the payment for the sinfulness of man, are resolved only by one person, Jesus Christ, and His sacrifice on the cross. When those are understood, the gospel is esteemed and treasured. It also should heighten the urgency to share this marvelous hope. The hope we have in the gospel. Once thoroughly understood, it should become the central mission of the church, and for individual believers! (As we will explore in later chapters) Helping people resolve interpersonal issues is important, but pales in comparison, in light of eternity.

Therefore, without a doubt, this is the ultimate question for each individual. The question for all time, because it determines our place for eternity. Either God is or He is not. Either He is eternally and intrinsically and immutably holy, or we have a defective and less than perfect God. Truthfully, those thoughts used to terrify me, knowing that I could have entered a state of eternity, and there would have been no recourse, or hope of ever escaping His absolute and perfect eternal justice. There are no adverbs that fully describe this potential reality. But notice the tense of my words. I "used" to fear this pending judgment, a literal Hell. I have now come to this full assurance of my salvation. Because, I have accepted the full salvation, given to me, via my faith/ trust in the payment of my sin, by my fully qualified Savior. I am now resting on the fact that God, who cannot lie, has made this promise. I can, therefore, forever rejoice in the assurance of my given salvation.

(A reflection) This is also the key consideration for teaching the security of the believer. If I am not permanently saved, then this concern for my eternal destiny, will be a recurring potential issue that will come up again. A potential that I need to be fearful about. Because I may be safe now, but there is no assurance that I may not have to face this dilemma of unresolved sin in the future, if in fact, I am not eternal and securely saved. (This too will be explored more in the coming chapters)

This message of salvation is historic Christianity. It is Biblical Christianity. We can deny it. We can ignore it. I have considered that option. Too heavy to keep in mind. Too unpleasant to consider. But I would need to abandon the faith, and by abandoning the faith, I would give up all hope. Furthermore, I would lose any meaningful reason for living, since I would still die one day. And my leaving the faith would not change whether it is true or not. It only removes the consideration from my mind. I actually think I would be freer. But it is a denial of truth, and reality. No matter how unpleasant the thought, it is the paramount of reality, it is the truth!

Now let's continue to consider the original salvation litmus test that I used in my class. This test opens our understanding of God's holiness and the completeness of Christ's salvific work on the cross. God cannot tolerate or accept anything short of perfect. He cannot, because to do so would compromise His intrinsic nature, and compromise would be to change His standards, and that defies His immutability, and intrinsic eternal holiness. (Again, being intentionally redundant, since this is one of the major premises of the book) This is eternity we are discussing. Our eternity! And our only hope! I really do not believe I can overdue emphasizing this subject!

1. The difficulty using particular references for these chapters is that this information has been found in dozens and dozens of books that I have read. I used a generalization of all that material. Please check out the Bibliography. In general they all address the same salvation themes.

CHAPTER 11

The Gospel Message

In our conception we inherited a sin nature. We sin because we are by nature, sinners. The evidence for this is any two year old child or teenager. In my case, a simple evaluation of my life. I sinned because-I did so naturally. Actually, when I am honest, I would say there were many times I enjoyed my sins. I later regretted most of them, but at the time they were desirable, or why would we do them. Additionally, God's revealed nature also magnifies my awareness of my sinfulness. This is part of the reason for the law. To define sin. To give an awareness of our sinfulness. Some reflective way to have a measurement of a standard. When we come under conviction via the work of the Holy Spirit, generally through the word of God, I have an initial understanding of my need. I am a sinner but God is not! Therefore, the obvious need for a personal Savior, a deliver. Someone who is able to rescue us from our sin penalty delima. We need someone that can meet our needs, if there is such a person? Thankfully, there is one, who is fully qualified. His name is a name above all names, the Lord Jesus Christ.

There are a host of things God does for the believing sinner to qualify him/her for heaven. (always remembering that one must be positionally perfect to be in the presence of God) Therefore, the absolute need of the cross, and the application by the Holy Spirit of those benefits. I will not give an exhaustive overview of those necessary requirements, but enough to bring confidence to the believer, so the one coming to faith, can rest assured, that all requirements necessary for entrance into heaven have been met. That every demand of the required justice before God has been fully satisfied by Jesus Christ. Which should result in peace to those who believe. A confidence that I am forever right with God. That the struggle to measure up to the standard has been fully satisfied. The uncertainty of my eternal future is now assured, that is, SHOULD I BELIEVE, AND PERSONALLY ACCEPT WHAT JESUS DID FOR ME ON THE CROSS, THE MESSAGE OF THE GOSPEL!

Before going too far with the requirements for salvation, I should indicate that we have a qualified Savior. If we need a complete salvation, we need a Savior who is completely qualified, and Jesus Christ is such. He is the eternal God, just as is God the Father. Actually, His deity is the basis, and the foundation for our salvation. (John 1:1-2, John 8:24) He was born via a virgin by the name of Mary, without the help of a biological father. He was conceived by the Holy Spirit in Mary. (This information for those who do not know the basic Christmas story) He eternally existed and only added human nature at conception. He is the exact representation of the eternal self existent God, God the Father. (Hebrews chapter 1) By being a man, He could stand in our place as a human, our representative. He therefore can be a Kinsman redeemer. An idea that one can stand in the place of another, because they/He has legal rights as a member of a group. (Ruth chapter 4) In this case, Jesus humanity gives Him standing as a representative of mankind. As fully God, He could make a payment, an atonement for sin, that was infinite in value. This is why the genealogies of the Gospels of Matthew and Luke are so significant. One gives His legal rights and the other gives His birth rights to be our substitute. Our Kinsman redeemer. Our qualified sinless Savior. Fully God and fully man in one person. This is the message, the Son of God became man, so by faith in His payment on the cross, we could become sons and daughters of God. We become children of our Heavenly Father.

His life proved His sinlessness. (Just read the four gospels) He is qualified to be the bridge to our needs. (Although, I don't fully like the bridge idea, since it may imply a need for me to do something, i.e. walk. While in the gospel, it is God who prepares a bridge, and He crosses it to us. Since Christ was the one that came to the earth and resolved our needs on the cross) Jesus Christ's sacrificial payment is the only, and the full, satisfaction of God's requirements of justice. When God the Father accepted the anticipated, and then completed sacrifice, which Christ proved was acceptable, by resurrecting from the dead. God was forever satisfied with the payment. A once for all time payment. Never to be repeated. Never needing to be repeated. A sacrifice of infinite value. We have an infinitely righteous Savior who was able to atone for all sins of all time. (Just read the NT epistles)

This was verified by His resurrection, witnessed by hundreds, and written about by those who meet with Him after his death. And, as a little apologetics, the fulfillment of hundreds of prophecies and types in the Old Testament, which predicted the mission on which He was sent. (Jesus confirmed this in Luke 24:25-27) Which is nearly mathematically impossible to be a happenstance. (Again there are better able scholars who will defend this statement. See some of the suggestions at the end of this book)

Now believing is the only acceptable response that God honors or accepts. Knowledge about Jesus is not enough. Knowledge is the understanding that an airplane can fly. Faith is the understanding, not only can airplanes fly, but that I get on the plane. I trust that belief. This is "a" definition of faith. A trust that gets me on the plane. Faith may come with some apprehension, but is trusting what I believe to be true, in that apprehension. There is no contribution that anyone can make that is acceptable to God, outside of accepting what Jesus Christ has already accomplished. There is no action or deed that measures up to God's infinite standards. We simply trust/ believe the revelation of God, as revealed in His only book, the Bible. There is a clear, one and only requirement, that is to believe/ accept what Christ completed on the cross on our behalf. This is God's instruction and only requirement. To add anything to what God demands, or requires, is not acceptable. Seriously, think this through, what could an inherently sinful man/woman offer to God, that would be in any way acceptable to meet His standards. Never forgetting His standards which are a reflection of His immutable righteous attributes. My need is literally an infinite solution that only God could provide. We needed mercy and grace. There is a difference. Mercy is not getting what we deserve, that is, punishment for sin. Grace is a step beyond that, it is the giving of something we have not earned, but receive as a gift. A gift that God is offering by His gracious hand. We have grace upon grace in Christ Jesus. The gift of God is a grace gift. Unearned! Just received!

Upon believing in the person and work of Christ, I am given eternal life. By general understanding, eternal means forever and forever. I possess at the very moment of faith, the gift of eternal life. Now having been a probation officer for many years I understand what probation conditions are. This is not what John 3:16, 5:24 or 6:47, and so many other passages teach. I have at that very moment, eternal or everlasting life. The very life of God imputed to me. The descriptive words that God the Holy Spirit guided the writers of scriptures to use, have intended meaning. God means what He says. So let us keep this real simple, eternal is forever, and forever is eternal. If I could lose this received gift of eternal life, then it was not really eternal from the beginning. God our Father is not a probation officer, nor works in the probation department. (I will develop this more later in the book) It is a very simple message. And we would be wise to stay with what God requires and accepts. Do not add or subtract to what God says. That is what Eve did in the garden. The gift of God is eternal life. And it is received simply by accepting the payment Christ made on our behalf. And upon receiving it, it is a present possession, and lasts forever and forever. Pretty simple, right?

Another benefit of believing the gospel is we are born again. In the 3rd chapter of the Gospel of John, Jesus says this is an absolute requirement. One must be born again or born from above. Just like natural birth, this is a one time and non-repeatable event. One is never born again only to need to be born again again. There is not a hint of this ever being required a second time in the scriptures. This is a one time event that happens at the very moment of faith in the gospel. This birth gives one acceptance into the family of God. A forever acceptance! Now that knowledge alone should give a wonderful and restful peace. The knowledge that God has accepted me into His forever family. This concept is also described as regeneration. The concept of spiritual birth or renewal. New birth into a new family. These results are not two steps, but one act of faith, which results in numerous necessary benefits. Since faith has no merit, it is simply accepting what God has offered. A free salvation. God's Grace! This is also expressed in the formula, that either one is born twice (physical and spiritual), in which case they will only die once (physical), or people who are only born once (physical), will die twice (both physical and eternally).

Not only are we accepted by new birth, we are adopted into the family of God. The first gives me supernatural birth into the family. Our acceptance is further described as full adoption. Adoption is the given legal rights, as a son or daughter, into a family that they were not originally born into. But now having the same rights and standing as one who was born into the family. This is true since we were born as sinners outside the family of God. Born into Adam's sinful race. We are now, at the moment of faith, fully adopted into the very family of God. A member of the household of God. Full standing as a son or daughter into the family of God.

Another great truth of the salvation gift is justification. The cornerstone of the reformation. It has been said that justification is the idea, that it is as though I had never sinned. But I understand it a bit more than that. I see it as God's declaration, that He has declared me just in his sight. A legal term. A legal declaration of my righteous standing before the bar of God's justice. A perfect standing of righteousness before a perfect God. God is the ultimate Judge of the universe, and this is His declaration of me, upon my faith in Christ Jesus and His completed accomplishment on the cross. (Romans chapter 5 and 8)

These truths continue. In the first chapter of both of the books of Ephesians and Colossians, the Apostle Paul talks about the redemption, the forgiveness of sins. It is addressed in other places too, like Hebrews chapter 9, verse 12, where it is described as an eternal redemption. The understanding is that in Christ, we have been redeemed and forgiven. It is a relief of a problem we had, that is undeserved, just recieved. A freeing thought! The truth that the benefits of Christ's death on the cross, upon my faith in the person and work of Jesus Christ, are applied to me, and results in my secure redemption. His sacrificial death payment made those benefits mine upon acceptance. The purchase price was fully paid for me on the cross, and resulted in my eternal redemption, which made me His forever. The price has been paid, for all of us, have you accepted it? It is like an uncashed check, it has potential value, but its real value is only good upon cashing.

These truths continue. There is a theological truth called Propitiation. Which means God's righteousness has been satisfied. God is forever satisfied with what Jesus Christ did on our behalf. If we have partaken of those benefits, then God is forever satisfied. Nothing for us to do in regards to securing salvation. He did it all. We simply respond to the offer.

There is also a standing that is necessary for all mankind. That is the standing of absolute righteousness before God. Now at the very moment of faith, we are forgiven of all our sins, gifted with eternal life, accepted into the family by new birth, adopted into the family of God, redeemed by the blood of Christ, and justified before God. We are also clothed in the very righteousness of Christ. He who bore our sins now cloths us with His untarnished righteousness. I am in Christ and He is in me. His perfect righteousness has been granted as an imputed gift of righteousness. We are now clothed in the very righteousness of Christ. That knowledge should cause a shout of praise. Not that it is required.

I hope you have come to understand these marvelous truths. They need to be known and embraced. They are well taught from many gifted scholars. As I have learned from many, including those like Dr. Andy Woods, in his Soteriology series. (Found at SLBC Dr. Andy Woods, under Soteriology) That in Adam lineage we were all imputed with the sinfulness of the first man. His sinful nature is being passed on to each and every person. On the cross, Christ was imputed with all the sins, of all mankind, of all time. Upon believing, I have been imputed with the very righteousness of Christ. I have full and complete standing in the family of God. As mentioned, there are two aspects, one is adoption, and the other, new birth. It is an eternal standing and sonship. An absolutely secure and eternal salvation. Think about that before moving on. We often read a profound truth and then quickly move to the next thought. This is a thought that needs to be pondered, anchored into your soul, and kept in your mind. If you want the presence of God's peace, and have settled assurance, meditate for a moment on these truths. In Christ, I am as righteous as Christ, because I have been clothed in His righteousness. An imputed righteousness! Therefore, I have the right to be in the presence of the Holy God, because I am, in my new positional righteous standing. I am now fully accepted! These truths understood are the first step in real worship! Authentic worship! The creator God has accepted me into His forever family.

And you would learn, in a more thorough study of the scriptures, the many more blessings that are granted upon the acceptance of what God did in the person and work of Jesus Christ. What he accomplished because of His love for us. How He made us potentially acceptable to Himself. Now is the time, with what has been written, to ask, have you believed? Have you accepted what God did for you when He gave His only begotten Son for you? Have you accepted His gift of salvation? I truly hope so! Because His holy standards will never change. There is not another option for us or for God. He is immutable, and cannot change the standards, even God cannot do somethings! He cannot change His holiness standards just because He loves us. His love motivated Him to undertake this redemptive plan, but His holiness does not allow another option. He has accomplished His plan. He has made "the" payment for you in the person and work of Christ. There are no other options or solutions to our sin problem. He is holy and we are sinners. We cannot change our inherited sin nature, but thanks be to God, by being born again, He has when we are spiritually born again. Then at physical death, the old nature is forever gone, and we continue on in a state called glorification. Until then, we are simultaneously both sinners and saints. Sinners in some of our actions, in our flesh, but Saints by position, by new birth.

The redemptive plan for our salvation is finished. And our redemption is a great truth to keep firmly in our minds. He made us redeemable when He paid our sin debt. When we trust in Christ's finished work on the cross, we are then redeemed. His death is satisfying payment, and is forever completed, never to be done again, never needing to be done again! Therefore, upon believing, the aforementioned blessings, and many more are fully and freely granted to you! At the very moment of faith! And, upon receiving, are never needed to be repeated, to remain a forever child of the living God. Please, don't forgo the opportunity to believe! Now is the day to receive the offer of salvation. Now is the time to accept the most magnificent gift. The free gift from God! Accept the finished work of Jesus Christ on your behalf and join the forever family of the eternal God. Because the work of Christ is only potentially salvific. You must personally accept this for yourself. Then it is a reality! God has no grandchildren. Your eternity is dependent on this decision. Let this sink in. We understand what happened on the cross when we understand we deserve eternal Hell. Which is more terrifying than anything you could ever fear. But I will say it again, that will never ever happen, if we simply accept the gift of salvation the Lord offers. I am very intentionally being an evangelist now! That is the primary reason for the book. To share this hope. And hope in the Bible is the confident assurance of what has been promised. It is not a wishful hope but an assured hope. Let's now move forward to see the church's expected role in this divinely given responsibility to share this eternal hope. Not to do so denies the very faith we profess to believe. If we are Christians? This is Christianity! The hope of the gospel.

You may think that I am overdoing it with the repeated emphasis on a few particular themes. Yes, this is a book that is addressing the weakness within the body of Christ to really grasp the unapproachable holiness of God. But ultimately, it is a book, with the intent to bring hell-bound sinners into the family of God. This subject is just that eternally important. Furthermore, I am also trying to impress upon the reader the understanding that the gospel will be neglected, if we fail to grasp the full significance of what we profess to believe. While it is primarily an evangelisic theology book, it also evaluates the importance of living out our faith according to the sound teachings of Biblical theology. The Bible should be the foundational truth for the way we live as a Christian. There is also the theme that should permeate throughout the book that simply asks the question; what are the implications if it is true? While I am not trying to defend the faith through traditional apologetics, I am trying to force the reader to grasp the implications of Christianity being absolutely true. Since if Christainity is not a dependable depiction of absolute truth, then everything I write is a wasted read, and was a wasted time to write. Furthermore, life is lived as a vapor without actual meaning. Yet, if you conclude with me that the Christain faith is based on strong evidence, and it is! Then there is no more urgent message to proclaim than the hope of eternal life in the gospel of Jesus Christ. Therefore, this is ultimately a book that lays out the logical implications of something being true; God is immutably holy, and we need a complete solution to an eternal destination problem. This is best seen in verse 6, of chapter 14, in the Gospel of John. This is why I emphasized that verse in this book. It forces the reader to face the exclusive claim by Jesus Christ, that only He is the way of salvation. It clarifies the outworking of the litmus test. The claim that Jesus is fully qualified to save us from the deserved wrath to come. Since my conviction is that this is true, I am alleging that there needs to be a more robust evangelistic response to these truths, since these implications are really eternal. This is why my emphasis is on pushing the truth to its logical conclusions and reinforcing the central points.

Lastly, I have spent numerous Sunday mornings in worship service, then later go golfing or meet up with friends later in the week, and have this occasional habit of asking what the Sunday message was about. Often it is with those, with whom, I attend the same church. Only to have them struggle to remember the content. Often a very solid message, but no lasting impact. Therefore, if I want to make a few unforgettable key points, I need to come back to the central themes over and over to make sure it finds a place in our memory. Like a good coach or proficient instructor, who trains the fundamentals, so they are like second nature. Please keep on reading to better understand some of the reasons this truth is not impacting us, as suggested, by the significance of what has been discussed.

1. Dr. Andy Woods found at SLBC Andy Woods, The whole Soteriology series.
2. The difficulty using particular references for these chapters is that this information has been found in dozens and dozens of books that I have read. I used a generalization of all that material. Please check out the Bibliography. In general they all address the same salvation themes.

CHAPTER 12

The call of the church to be proclaimers of truth

The church has been boxed in by society, by those who do not hold to our Biblical perspective. There are many voices in our society who desire the church to limit its influence to the mission of compassion outreach. Where the primary mission is to care for the poor and less fortunate in our society. There certainly is a place in the mission of the church for compassionate care for the needy. The Bible teaches that principle. (In the Old Testament, this principle is discussed, for example, in Deuteronomy, chapters 15 and 26. This compassion is also modeled throughout the New Testament) It also says that those who do not work, should not eat. And, if a man does not care for his family, he is worse than an unbeliever. I think we can take that as a universal principle even though it was written to believers in the church. And its direct application is to define a standard for believers who want to be in good standing in their local fellowship. There is a Biblical expectation for believers to care for and love their families. The wider application is that this addresses a significant problem in our communities today, and many men in particular need to step up, and be engaged fathers. Intact families are the anchor for healthy neighborhoods. Too many men seem much better at procreation of children than nurturing them into responsible adulthood. Any mindless person can get a woman pregnant. It is the abandonment of the responsibilities of fatherhood that is the problem. But that is not the theme of this chapter. Just a little soup box commentary. Let's return to the topic of this chapter.

A secular society will accept a church that does not stir its moral conscience. So as long as we compromise our values, our evangelsitc mission, and remain focused on charitable activities, we are acceptable. Maybe even valued for our charitable work. At least tolerated without too much objection. Just don't take a moral stand, or try to influence society regarding moral standards. Certainly do not suggest non-Christians are lost and engage in evangelism. How insensitive to suggest people are morally accountable to God, and therefore need a Savior. Take care of the poor, the hungry, and leave morals to be defined by those in the political arena, the academic halls of learning, or holywood. Good grief, how is that working for us?

Unfortunately, this has been the appeal to the masses, by many in mainline denominations. Acceptability of all, with few of the expectations of Biblical morality. In particular, those standards of conduct, in regards to their sexual morality. The expected morality that should emanate from the faith, into the lives of those who proclaim to be Christians. This altering of long-standing sexaul morality has a certain appeal to those who do not hold to our Biblically based perspectives. Where love is king of all virtues. Let's just love people as they are without too many moral expectations. The belief held in this moral vacuum, is if love is a true emotion, we should not question whether it is moral behavior. (We should always be expressions of authentic love, without compromising our values)

This drift from Biblical truth also includes the compromising teaching that one can be heaven bound, and not even accept the fundamentals of the faith. (Fundamentals are just accepting the faith as being true. These are not radical extreme unbiblical actions) That is not Christianity! It is like, I am a Christian, but wink wink, I don't really believe it is fundamentally true. For those who hold to this view, there are elements of the faith that appeal to them, the acts of kindness and expression of love. The community of fellowship. A God-ness, but not Biblical Christianity. They promoted the theology that general goodness, and expressions of love, will ultimately satisfy God's requirements. Love wins in their minds. Unfortunately, this is not true, love wins when we accept it on God's terms, and that requires the cross! This modified message of Christianity, is not the same message propagated by their founders. This is a form of progressive thinking Christianity, but not Biblical Christianity. It is a redefining of Christianity.

Think for a moment of Jonathan Edwards famous sermon, "Sinners in the hand of an angry God". Or, the traveling evangelist with a burning passion, traveling across the country sharing a fire and brimstone message, warning sinners of the judgment to come. Or, the bold, and life changing faith, of the Wesley brothers, Charles Finney, D. L. Moody and George Whitefield. Their profound impact on our county, because of the strong moral values that emanate from their preaching, that helped us become a great nation. Not sure those fire and brimstones messages are an effective way to preach in today's culture, but there is a sentiment to what they preached. A bit of a missing ingredient in today's church that has an, I am alright, and you're alright, mentality. A little return to those more direct confrontational preaching styles, may help us return to what's really important. Remember, real revival starts with prayer, and is composed of a renewed sense of the holy. A perception of God's righteous anger toward sin. A revival in our county will not happen in the environment that espouses a watering down of Biblical standards. Actually, no revival starts with solf on truth theology, we need hard truth. God is an immutable holy truth. It is not the learning of some newly discovered truth that starts a revival. It comes when something we knew was true, is taken as uncompromisingly true, like John 14:6! This was seen in the Reformation, which started with a renewed understanding of justification by faith alone, and that the Bible was the sole authority for truth. On these truths, and a few more, became their deep convictions, that those Reformers who would not back down on! This was the impetus for the beginning of restoring the truths of Biblical Christianity.

Regretfully, the truth of the matter is, most mainline churches have fundamentally drifted far from the orthodoxy of the faith. And that growing movement has even drawn the evangelical church in that direction. Some churches are even endorsing gay marriage, and performing those ceremonies within the church. Abandoning even the basics of Christian sexual morality. We recently had a pastor in our communtiy who offered to perform gay marrigages for free at a local coffee house. I am sure he found acceptable interest within the liberal church community. A real hero of progress to many. Not sure he had God's blessing on the whole situation.

(And, yes, that was sarcasm) It is noteworthy that while mainline churches have found more acceptability with those outside the Biblical perspective, those who like a benevolent mission of the church, but who only give a superficial nod to the traditional beliefs of their denominational fathers, they have in the process lost the sure message of eternal hope.

And while the trend to a more liberal theology has allowed them to avoid the stigma for previously, and strongly held beliefs, the end result is they have lost much of their impact. Their influence for moral good has greatly suffered. Those churches have clearly lost much of the powerful impact first achieved by their founders and early followers. Those who started movements, that created whole new denominations, that we still recognized in our communities. Those deeply held passions are now greatly lost in this time of so-called progress. Or, what is seen as progress by many. A progresive Christian faith. Free from the stigma of past convictions inherent in Biblical truth. Where now sexual preferences can be chosen by the individual, and endorsed by society, and often by their church bodies. (I want to be careful here. I want to be very clear! Kindness and Christian respect for the dignity of our fellow man/women is still expected by those of us who do not agree with this moral drift. Grace, love and truth all together, is the model)

Furthermore, as we see the deviation from Biblical truths continued, so did their numbers, and declined significantly. The more they abandoned the Biblical standards of their founders, and the more socially receptive they found themselves with those outside the church, the less impactful they became. These are those, who are comfortable with the benevolent mission of the church, but reject the necessary salvific aspect of the faith. They abandoned many of those moral expected standards that have historically been identified, as a reflection of being a good Christian. The belief was that this opening up, and being more flexible with alternative lifestyles, would make them more appealing. They had reasoned that by being more accepting of the societal values that are constantly changing, and adjusting their own to blend in, they would be more attractive to outsiders. Some of these compromising values included; embracing the teaching of evolution, the avoidance of the subject of hell, denying hell, and lowering the standard of those alleged outdated sexual expectations. Their hope was erroneously held. They had hoped that by adapting these changing values, they would draw the outsiders in, thereby growing the church in unqualified love for mankind. The opposite has happened. Many of the insiders have left for the outside, oftentimes, to churches that still held to traditional Biblical morality. (I did) The decline of the mainline church has been significant. Even the faithful segments of the church who remained, who found comforting of conscience with the softening of doctrine, now seem lost as to what to believe. Even loss as to what their ultimate purpose is. What they failed to understand, is when the church leaves its strong doctrinal foundation, they no longer have real truth. They lost their anchor. Leaving them adrift, without Biblical prescription for why they even exist.

Be sure, there are true believers in those bodies, and many wonderful people. I grew up in a mainline church. I love those people. I think experientially, I could find fellowship there, that is comfortable, and humanly satisfying. They are good natured people. They are known as kind and compassionate people. Very welcoming. If only I could set aside my belief in the inerrancy of the Bible, and the absolute necessity for personal salvation to name a few. Which I cannot do, because of the ramifications of what happens when we do! A logical breakdown of this thought process is discussed as we progress through the remainder of the book.

(Some reflections) Early on in my faith journey, there came a period of reflection in my own life, as I started to evaluate the mainline church's message and focus. I observed how much it had been reduced to; God is love, love all people, and care for the poor. Granted, there is some value in that message. God is a God of love. We are to help care for the poor. But it is woefully incomplete, and misses the main focus and call of the church of Jesus Christ. It also diminishes the whole reason and purpose for the death of Christ. In light of eternity, this acceptance of the compromised message leaves well fed, but eternally lost souls. We should be a place of fellowship that is accepting, and meaningful, but in the process we cannot ignore the foundations of our faith, or the gospel message, the truth of what we have historically believed. Because when we blend in to fit in, we lose our significance. The standard of truth. We are no longer the salt and light. We become irrelevant as professed believers. Just soup kitchens. We become connected with some segments of society, but disconnected with ultimate truth.

(Some more observations) I like, from a human perspective, that theme song for the show, Cheers. It included a verse, "A place where everyone knows your name". A place of acceptance and friendship. Over a few beers they shared their lives and enjoyed fellowship, and a lot of laughter at the end of a stressful day. It was a place they fit in. They experienced life together. They laughed together. There's something appealing to that. Who does not want to feel like they belong? That we have people with whom to share our lives. A place where we feel valued and accepted. Some hearty laughter and good will. Good fellowship and a feeling that we do belong. Unfortunately, many churches often progress little more than that, they just add a little spirituality to the fellowship. Yet it lacks what is the primary call for the church, to be the salt and light, and truth bearers of God's message. For the evangelical church to remain true to its calling, it should create a welcoming environment, a place of authentic fellowship. (Maybe without the beer. Go ahead and smile, a little humor does not hurt) Yet without the loss of Biblical truth. Where, when referring to ourselves as evangelicals, means we evangelize. And we stand on the fundamentals of what we profess to believe. Because without actual Biblical truth, we are adrift in irrelevance.

Notwithstanding the need for authentic fellowship, when the church leaves its greater call, it loses its unique value. It becomes a social club. Regrettably, I think this is becoming too universal across the scope of the Western church. The Americanization of the church. Where we confuse Christianity with the so-called American dream. We all naturally prefer personal comfort, stimulating music, and preaching that is focused on personal improvement. We prefer chasing the vaper of the good life. There is a normal desire to want our lives to be rich, and find satisfaction in this life. Me too, but not at the cost of denying the truthfulness of the Biblical Gospel, which is the only hope for eternal satisfaction. If we deny essential truths? What do we have? Soup kitchens!

I am seeing it a bit too often, even in evangelical churches. Here are a number of recurring themes I have noticed. How to get along with difficult people. How to have a healthy attitude. How to find personal peace. How to deal with conflict and emotional issues. How to move past those areas of life that are holding us back from inner peace. Teaching the body of believers how to deal with negative emotions keeps people coming back. There is a saying, preach to where people are hurting, and you will always have an audience. There are certainly significant numbers of these individuals in the body of Christ. Those that have been overwhelmed by the hurts of life. We live in a broken society that needs this restorative help. This is worth preaching and teaching and mentoring. It is also an area where mature believers should mentor newer believers in the faith. (Remember Matthew 28:19-20 and the pastoral letters of Titus and Timothy) We need to have mature, well ground, and seasoned saints for this to be a practical reality. But is this the foremost purpose and divine depiction of the local church? In light of eternity! This needs to be a sure component of a health church, but not the main cornerstone.

See if this illustration helps. Let's say one day after shower you see a mark on your skin. Being a bit concerned you have it checked out at the Dermatologist. After examination, he assures you that it is normal, and nothing to be concerned about, all part of the aging process. You are thankful that this mild concern is nothing to be seriously concerned about. Then sometime later you start experiencing pain in your side. You wisely decide to have it checked out by a doctor. After extensive testing he has very disturbing news. It is advanced cancer and you have very little time to live. Naturally you are devastated. You have been told there is no treatment and death is in your near future. Later sharing your devastating news with a friend, he informs you, there is a new breakthrough treatment just discovered. You see this new doctor, and he assures you that this information is true. There is a revolutionary new, and 100% proven treatment, just approved for use. Your response is now different. Instead of mild relief you are ecstatic with the revealing news. The point is this, the church treats our situation of being lost like a mild skin blemish, and not a revolutionary and life saving treatment, one that is eternally life saving. This is the spiritual quest that we all face. Not just a temporary extension of life, or an improved way to live, but an eternal solution to our hopelessness, before the ultimate justice of a holy God.

In light of eternity, we need to keep the main thing the main thing. A constant reminder to us individually and as a corporate church body. The reminder that the gospel solution to man's ultimate need, is one that necessitates it being preached regularly from the pulpits, and preached with urgency and accuracy. There is only one divinely given salvific message. And because of the eternal consequences, it needs to be thoroughly known, articulated, and proclaimed in all its details. Otherwise people will go on their frolicsome way oblivious to the consequences ahead. Believing that they are meritorious on their own. Good and decent people we want as neighbors, but are not born again children of God. These unsaved are in a precarious position, since they are baselessly depending on their own insufficient righteousness, never having the perfect righteousness that God's justice demands. And, sadly when this is realized, it will be too late.

One of my frustrations with the church today is the over emphasis on some of the less-essentials, or avoiding the hard truth of the faith, to avoid the stigma of the harder truths of the faith. Sorry to say, but many pastors will receive a strong rebuke from the Lord at the Judgment Seat of Christ. They were not faithful with the commission of the gospel, or were inaccurate in its presentations. (Galatians 1:8-9) Many of those who sit under their ministries are falsely mistaken on what is required for entrance into the heavenly abode. Not exactly watchmen on duty. This is becoming a growing problem within the modern evangelical church. Where are the voices of pastors? Generally more concerned about the world's opinion. Looking for acceptance with the world. They are too often misguided in the essentials of the gospel. Some pastors are even denying the fundamentals of the historical faith. Those aspects of the faith that allow the gospel to be known and properly responded to.

The pulpits are abandoning truth to find acceptability with the masses. This is compounded by the drift of our Christian colleges into modernism where pastors are often trained. Particularly, when it comes to the standard of the inerrancy of the scriptures, traditional salvation doctrines, traditional marriage, and compromising acceptance of evolution, all of which results in a diminished church. When this takes place, it naturally results in churches forgoing the urgency to proclaim eternal hope, the gospel of Jesus Christ.

This modernism of the church is manifesting in the shabby state of our churches. That is slowly becoming a mirror of our communities. I believe there are many reasons for leaving the Biblical mandate. Here are a few for reflection. #1. We are being boxed in by the expectations of society. #2.

We fail to grasp the seriousness of God's holiness. #3. The consequences of eternity are hard to emotionally accept. #4. The social discomfort of evangelism is unappealing to most believers. #5. There is pressure to accept evolution as true in order to have perceived acceptability with the intellectuals of our day. #6. The inability to defend the scriptures as the infallible standard of truth. #7. The unwillingness to accept that for the most of humanity, heaven is not their destination. #8. That Hell is real and is a real consequence for rejecting the loving offer from God.

Certainly there is strong societal pressure to adopt the world's standards. Evangelism is still an activity that I don't particularly care for. What an odd thing to do, unless, Christianity is true. Then it is the most compassionate and critical activity to undertake as a Christain. (I still don't care for it) But the status of the lost demands this be of the highest priority. We get to this place in our churches when we compromise the truth. This leads us back to the need to understand the immutable holiness of our God. Which when understood, should lead to an urgency, to share this sure hope we have in the Gospel.

When the church becomes more acceptable to the world, it becomes more insignificant in purpose and call. Consequently, it loses God's message of salvation to a dying world in the process. I understand emphasizing this in many churches will cause some to leave for a more comfortable church in which to fellowship. There they can find worthy projects of helping the poor, and still find acceptability with the world. Or, they may just walk away. They may even be eternally saved and forever a member of the family of God, but refused to take the next step in discipleship. They may simply avoid the divine call to engage others with the message of hope. Some of Jesus' disciples did when He put forth hard truths. But, by doing so, we are denying the essential truths that make Christianity, Biblical Christianity. By abandoning the truth of the immutable God, they have created their own version of God, that is not reflected in the scriptures. For those who are truly saved, there will be consequences. There is a coming assessment for all believers at the Bema seat of Christ. (More on that in chapter 21)

One of the hardest things about the covid period was the loss of fellowship. The ability to disciple and support fellow believers. We are created to experience fellowship. (I am glad this period appears to be passing) To share together corporate worship and reaffirm what we proclaim as the truth. (This is so true in my own life) In the meantime, what better time to engage in the great mission given to the church. When people are so uncertain about the direction of life. This is more than finding personal peace and satisfaction in this life. It was not the primary mission for the Apostle Paul. While he wrote about many of these sanctification issues, it was not his driving passion. (read the 20th chapter of Acts) He abandoned everything to get out the gospel. That only made personal sense if the message was absolutely true.

He writes analytically about that priority in 1st Corinthians, chapter 15. If the resurrection is not true, then everything he did spreading the gospel was a wasted effort. That any sacrifice of personal comfort was for not. (my paraphrases) In the event the resurrection did not happen, then Christianity is not true, then the agreed upon arrangement in my marriage illustration in chapter 4, does make some sense, destructive sense, but logical sense. But even in that scenario we still die someday. Is sex and personal comfort meaningful enough reason to live? Studies show the opposite. Those who enjoy the most rewarding and meaningful sex lives are those who develope them in an exclusive married relationship. Without the guilt and regret that comes from those alleged freedoms. A standard that is being lost in the body of Christ. That a lifetime relationship that is nurtured in love and faithfulness, is really the best foundation, and most meaningful way to live. So it really comes back to the question; is Biblical Christinaity true? That truth determines my actions.

CHAPTER 13

God command for the church to fulfill the great commission

I am contending in this book that we are failing to grasp the weight of the unapproachable holiness of God. That it is a vastly neglected teaching in our churches. Most will accept the basic premise that God is holy, but the full implications of God being absolute holy is a different matter. They grasp that God is holy, but neglect to give that truth its natural implications. For example, when it comes to the urgency of evangelism, there are a growing number of professed believers who now believe there are other means of entering the heavenly abode. Many Christians (Those who identify themselves as Christians) now believe one can enter the heavenly abode via another religion. The understanding of the exclusivity of Christ alone is being compromised. This is because they fail to grasp the full significance of the litmus test I previously gave in chapter 10. This is the reason why I used my litmus test. It clarifies for an individual, whether they are understanding of the unmitigated holiness of God, and sufficiency of Christ's work on the cross. It defines the issue. If there is another way, then, Christ died in vain. (Remember John 14:6 and 1st Corithians chapter 15) Resulting in Christianity being reduced to secondary benefits like feeding and clothing the poor.

That is why the understanding of the immutable holiness of God, while understandably uncomfortable to consider in its full ramifications, is absolutely crucial to the Great Commission given to the church. (Matthew 28:19-20) For without this knowledgement, the church loses its motivation to pursue its primary mission, to reach the lost with the Gospel of Jesus Christ. The litmus test reaffirms that there is only one hope. There is only one name that is able to save. (Acts 4:10-12, particularly verse 12) But this is not generally the mindset of today's progressive church, which has often denied the exclusivity of the faith.

For most, to consider the status of the lost is too agonizing to even ponder in today's culture, so it is replaced with more palpable messages. There is growing pressure on pastors to provide more desirable messages, those messages that massage the conscience, but avoids the inherent truths, which then clouds the church to eternal irrevency. For without the litmus test, we may start to believe we are all acceptable to God, which diminishes the value of what Jesus accomplished on the cross. This neglect for what is true about God's nature, results in a growing disinterest for the subject of evangelism, which has eternal repercussions. This results because most people do not want to face their own mortality, or explore the reality of what happens at death, so the thoughts are suffocated in the back of their minds. Consequently, the pursuit of the implications of who Christ is, or what He actually accomplished by His death on the cross, is either denied, diluted or ignored. Most evangelicals profess as a doctrine they believe, but dilute the implications. Whereas progressives deny the exclusivity of salvation, based on the merits of Christ alone, but continue to practice a shadow of the truth, which is no truth at all.

Notwithstanding these thoughts, considering the implications of the gospel message, evangelism should be the most urgent mission of the church. For those of us who claim the name of Christ, if the faith is true, and it is, should make this the premier priority.

There is a journal entry by the late missionary, Jim Elliot, that reads, "He is no fool who gives what he cannot keep to gain what he cannot lose". That principle could be applied to monetary usage of resources, knowing that upon death, they have no remaining value to the owner. Or, in the ultimate evanglisic service for the Lord, since there is nothing we can take with us beyond the grave, besides those eternal investments. So investing your life for what will last forever, is the most perspicacious manner in which to live. Jim Elliot believed that principle to the point that it cost him his life on the mission field.

Unfortunately, this is not the present mindset of the average believer today. According to a 2008 Pew Research, and many other polls, a majority of Christians now believe that people can reach heaven apart from the gospel message. That belief is irreconcilable with the historical understanding of Biblical Christianity. The gospel that Jesus, the Apostle Paul and the others taught. And is one of the mainsprings that should flow from the understanding of the absolute immutable holiness of God. The cornerstone of the Biblical faith. Should we conclude that Apostle Paul's evangelistic motivation, was a rational response, based on the compelling evidence for the actual physical resurrection of Christ, as described in the Gospels, written about in his epistles and the book of Acts, and his grasping the eternal significance of its ramifications, then that same response should be more pronounced in our church ministries.

I know most will naturally be uncomfortable with its implications in their personal lives. They desire to be good people. That is noble. We should be good people. But prefer not to have it emphasized too much in their places of worship. It is too agonizing for most to even consider. Many do not want to admit this is the truth of what we profess to believe. So we ignore the implications. Truthfully, that is my preferred comfort level too. I have a desired life I want to live and experience, but to live in such a manner, would require that I deny the essence of the faith. Or, I diminish the faith, and serve a less than perfectly holy and immutable God, who will not extract perfect justice. Not exactly a God that exudes the worship in Revelation or Isaiah, the fall on your face, overwhelmed by His majesty.

Therefore, this neglect to perceive God's intrinsic nature has created a lukewarm church. The more we drift from a reliable and solid biblical comprehension, the more insignificant the church. The church loses its eternal and distinctive message of hope. It is obvious that the church has drifted significantly over the decades. What once were churches strongly established on truths contained in the scriptures, comprehending the eternal consequences of the proclaimed faith, have now been replaced by the spiritual mystic experience. Where the terrestrial interest has taken priority over those with eternal ramifications. One of the first aspects of the church's mission to suffer neglect is the priority of purpose driven evangelism. The weight of this has now been replaced with social programs and those of self-help. Which are more appealing to many congregations.

Those actions feel good and avoid the stigma. Therefore, over focusing on the temporary quality of one's life, to the neglect of the eternal, resulting in a practice of our faith that is often void of eternal value.

Be sure, the Bible gives a Chrisitian a roadmap for how to live a meaningful life, addressing every conceivable aspect of life. If one wants a good foundation for living a meaningful life, Christianity is the best place to start. Since every conceivable aspect of life is taught in the Bible. However, no matter how one computes the value of a meaningful life, always remember that every temporary pursuit in this life has an ending point, it is fleeting, since the way of all men is death. Therefore, if there is one question that absolutely must be resolved before entering the state of eternity, it is not the quality of your life, or what you were able to accomplish outside of Christ, it is making sure of one's eternal destiny, and then living a life of eternal significance. Only the Bible is a reliable source for how to be assured of heaven and how to avoid Hell. Then subsequently, how to live an eternally relevant life, and what is required for this to be realized in each person's life. The Bible is the only book that addresses these subjects in a reliable manner. Both the temporary, and more importantly, the eternal. And this neglect of understanding is being manifested in the priorities of the weekly church worship service. This exclusive truth of the litmus test is not being proclaimed.

Whereas, the great commission is the urgency of bringing the assurance of eternal hope, to a terminal world, and therefore, it should be the premier priority for the church. The sanctification of the believer follows. Which too. is an aspect of the great commission, the development of mature disciples of Christ. The changing of the world, one person at a time through evangelism, and then personal discipleship. Unfortunately, this is generally nowhere to be found in many bodies of believers. Where are the deeply mature believers who are able to minister individually to those in the body? First, equipt to bring the lost to saving faith, then grounded in the faith, so they can help disciple men and women into seasoned and effective duplicating saints. Chrisitans who are able to teach the word and disciple effectively. This story of our redemption should become our ministry of sharing with others the way of redemption.

I believe if we want effective and mature believers, interpersonal issues need to be addressed and worked through. It is part of making people whole and well rounded saints. When this desired aspect of discipleship, which should be part of the mission of the church, is lacking, then so are mature saints. So please don't understand me here. I am not indicating the present struggles should be ignored. I am suggesting that an over emphasis of pursuing temporary success, to the neglect of the eternal, is foolish in light of eternity. When these take too much priority, the church compromises its greater call, to reach the lost with the ultimate hope, the Gospel of Jesus Christ.

The issue remains, that this life is temporal. No escaping that reality. Upon death, there is no recourse to our condition. If anyone neglects the free offer of salvation, there is no second chance. Seems to me to be a foolish consequence that I am not willing to risk. I want that absolute assurance of what the eternal future holds. As often been noted, we will spend considerable time planning our once in a lifetime vacation, but ignore a once in lifetime event that has eternal consequences. The implications of the undeniable, and inescapable truth of our pending death, is a reality that we can not ignore. We will make diligent efforts to make sure our retirement is secure, not even knowing if we will be alive to enjoy it. I have known dear friends who spent a lifetime securing a stable and promising retirement, only to die prematurely and pass on those benefits to someone who did not earn them. This too is vanity. Again, read the book of Ecclesiastes, which looks at the vanity of the temporal pursuits, with a God-centered view of life.

I have often heard church leaders discuss their frustration with the lack of involvement by the members in their local body of believers. It is a true observation. There are at least three issues I believe contribute to this situation. The first, is in many ways, the body does feel there are two tiers of ministry. Those of the paid and then the volunteers. The paid have clerical support and resources available to them that are often needed for lay ministers too. The leadership in the church needs to focus on the teaching of priesthood of all believers. And welcome the more mature believers into roles that elevate them to teaching and sometimes preaching, provided those are their gifts. The idea that there is a mountain of Biblical wisdom that has only been achieved by the paid is a fallacy. I have found many well read and gifted believers that are not being utilized or developed to their fullest. They are artificially being held back because it is believed they are not qualified for some ministerial responsibilities, because they do not have the official title of pastor. But even in the pastoral books of the Bible, the elder is one who must be able to teach the doctrines of the faith. If that is a requirement to be an elder, then it is also a responsibility, or an opportunity that should be afforded to those so gifted. No one man is the source of all knowledge or spiritual insight. One pastor preaching week in week out as though he is the only fountain of Biblical wisdom, may not be the best use of a body's talent. No one man is that deep in endless knowledge. We are a body of believers, each with different skills and abilities, that should be better utilized.

The second, is pastors have done an inadequate job of teaching maturing believers how to be duplicating ministers of the gospel. The message we have needs to be taught to others with the desired effect, that they too, can minister to individuals in their unique contact situations. Pastors don't have the board access to the unsaved masses that the congregational members often do through their work, business or other natural contacts. This diminishes the expansion of the gospel into their communities. (This is a major focus in the book of Ephesians, chapter 4. The equipping of the saints for the ministry) Preaching to the body is not discipleship. Sunday school or Wednesday night services are not discipleship if they are not training sessions. Part of discipleship is duplicating mentorship, one generation to the next. The equipping of the present generation to carry the message forward, then equipping the next in the fundamentals of the faith. This was a big theme in both Testaments. By various means, believers were called to be ambassadors of the faith, by passing on the truths of the faith, once for all given. (See the book of Jude)

This leads to the third factor affecting the lack of growth in the body. Where are the mature discipled believers who are able to mentor the hurting. If there are marriage issues? Where are the successful and stable partners who are able to mentor the young, but struggling couples. It is certainly a principle that Apostle Paul discussed in his pastoral letters to Timothy and Titus. This applies to both men and women with some conditions. Older women teaching younger women on how to be good mothers and wives. Men teaching men on how to man up and be stand up men of the faith. How to love their wives. Personal discipleship was the practice of Jesus. Discipling men in the faith who later became apostles and evangelists. Principle upon principle with the goal of maturing the faith in new believers, then duplicating the faith to the next generation.

It needs to start as a priority in the pulpits. If pastors want to be a mature and multiplying ministry, it needs to create that emphasis. Setting forth the principle that this is the mission of the church. Emphasizing that the gospel changes the eternal destiny of the unbeliever. The intentional engagement with the new believers, then mentoring them in the discipleship process. The taking of a babe in Christ, helping him become a mature and duplicating member of the local body. Anchored, and able to defend and proclaim the hope we have in Christ. This results in the greater part of the body having a mindset to be ministry orientated. At least it should be! This is the process of evangelism to discipleship the Bible lays out. Whole movements have started this way. Like the emergence of Sunday school programs, which now misses the mark of real discipleship making, and are now often just informational sessions. We have gone from the Great Commission to the great omission.

Think about the churches that are shadows of their past founders. The driving passion that gave rise to these denominations. Those, most often, having a burning desire to reach the lost. These churches have now become shadows of their past zeal. If we don't properly assess our declining situation as an evangelical church we are headed to irrelevance. We will be simply reduced to being soup kitchens. What once was a bright light of truth and gospel, that changed lives, is a community of well fed but lost souls. Our impact on the community is slowly becoming nothing more than a social support system. When the light of truth grows dim, so goes the society, manifesting in our communities in the form of moral decay. Sin has personal and community consequences. Shame from sin is a hard thing to live with. So are the resulting broken lives of those deceived by the allure of unrestrained sexual freedom. Only a clear understanding of the newness of life in Christ, can give the hope to start anew as a newly born saint. It starts with evangelism, then progresses in learning how to live out of our new identity as a child of the King. It starts with the gospel and continues in discipleship.

What greater call is there for the church than to bring the lost to Christ and then build them up in the faith. Equipping them so there is a lasting change in their personal lives, but also in their families. The unified effort to bring lost, and hell bound sinners, into a right standing with God. Seems so harsh and distasteful, but it is literally and Biblically true. I may feel a strong uneasiness with the idea. It is certainly something that I personally would prefer to ignore. But I am left with the recurring delima, either the faith is built on solid evidential foundations, or let's all eat and drink and be merry, because this transitory life is just that. Most will simply ignore it. Putting out of mind is easier. But we can't honestly justify that mindset when the litmus test is valid. The truth that God is absolutely holy, and the gospel is absolutely sufficient to save even the worst of sinners, remains true.

This is why I believe this message of this book is so needed today. It is not an easy book to write. I like my life for the most part. I have a nice marriage. I enjoy my time with our children and grandchildren. I have many good quality friends. I really don't care to be overtly evangelistic. Furthermore, I work in an environment that is very suspicious of "religion". The implications of the holiness of God is very unsettling for me. I don't desire to be continuously mindful of the nature of God's standards. I prefer a good God with flexible and adaptable values. It would be easier to live with. The fit in values. But that is not the God of the Bible. Therefore, the question remains; is it true or not? If not, then let's eat, drink and be merry, for tomorrow we die. I mean I am in my 60's. My life is starting to fade as the years go by. So the consequences still remain. Either give me the sure and confident word that is true, which results in a confident assurance of my eternal destiny, knowing that the best is yet to come. Or, give me a cold beer, and let's have a good time. Those who are strong foundamentalist may find objection with my last statement. But is it consistent with what the apostle Paul wrote in in 1ˢᵗ Corinthians chapter 15. If for this life only....

CHAPTER 14

Understanding our call to be evangelistically obedient

(Editorial note. As you read this chapter it may appear I am jumping back and forth with essentially the same contrasting thoughts. Wait until the end of the chapter and I will clarify why)

In the previous chapter, I discussed the churches need to make evangelism, then duplicating discipleship, the central part of the mission. (Matthew 28:19-20) This chapter is focusing on the exhortation by God, to each individual Christian, of our responsibility to fulfill the great commission. There should be an urgency for that mission to reach the loss with the gospel. When an Christian ponders the implications of eternity, personal evangelism should be the most natural response. And our degree of motivation reflects whether we are genuinely grasping a clear understanding of the consequences of the message. This is the case I have been making throughout the content of this book. There are the profound implications inherent in the gospel message of Christ's death and resurrections. Let's continue thinking this through.

Most individuals generally enjoy our annual religious traditions. They look forward to the seasonal celebrations of the birth of our Jesus Christ, and His death and resurrection. They are generally cherished traditions that bring a sense of meaning and times of personal reflection. A time to be together as family and friends. These are family traditions that have been passed on for generations. However, there seems to me, that there is an immense disconnect between the reality of these momentous events of history, and how much merit we give to them. It is almost like we don't grasp the significance of our celebrations, the real implications of being true. In our superficial celebrations of these holidays, we are in essence, denying the connotations of what we are celebrating.

For example, consider the importance of the resurrection of Christ. It may be the most important event in history. If actually true, then the implications have eternal repercussions. Far more than the fuzzy and warm seasonal celebrations, that these celebrations give rise to in the average American's life. This also is true for the birth of Christ. The idea that God Almighty entered humanity is far more significant than is really appreciated. This is logically confusing, if we are giving the weight of these events their due. I have spent considerable time pondering why this is so. It should be apparent we are failing to grasp the full inference of these momentous events of human history. The death of Christ, His resurrection and the entrance of God into humanity are not some insignificant events. They are events in human history that are of uttermost importance. May I suggest there are a number of factors that might explain why this is true.

The first is we have adapted a form of universalism. The idea being held by many Christians is that Chrisitanity is the best way but not the only way. Those that hold this view believe it will somehow work out for the others. Surely God did not mean a real literal Hell, and if He does, it is only for the most evil of mankind. (The Hitlers of the world) Or, we generally believe it may be true, but are not convinced. We often only go as far as our faith sustains us. We are not willing to sacrifice our present day pleasures for something that may not be entirely true. We hope it is true, but we are not absolutely sure. Another factor for some is simple disbelief. They like the traditions, but are suspicious of the truthfulness of Christainity. Lastly, some are simply caught up with living life, pursuing the good life, and the implications of our beliefs interfere with that desired life. They like some aspects of the celebrations, but they are blind to the actual significance of these events. In all these cases, people are not asking the most pertinent question, whether it is absolutely true or not. In all of these cases, it is clear they have never come to the point of weighing the magnitude of the claims of Jesus, as alleged in John 14:6. They never settled in their minds the real ramifications that are inherent, in the very claims of the exclusivity of salvation alone in Christ alone. His claim of deity. (John 8:24) But there are a few other factors too.

We believe in the plane's ability to fly but have not taken a seat on the plane. Meaning we have not exercised trusting faith. We may believe it is likely true, but have stopped short of trusting it personally as our only hope for eternity. Or, we reluctantly believe it is true, but don't like the implications, so we minimize it. We are embarrassed to admit to those outside the faith that this is what we believe. We lack the courage to stand on the fact that it is really really true. Lastly, we may believe we merit heaven with our faith and good works, a combination of our good deeds and God's grace. Therefore, the cross is minimized, because people believe they are somewhat earning heaven. Regardless of the reason, the impact of those events are devalued as to the full significance. Two and two do not equal four anymore. What we celebrate is not given its actual worth.

Regardless of these perspectives, an underappreciated faith does matter. What people know and believe is eternally significant. I know most non-fundamental Christains have various conceived ideas of how to gain entrance into this Kingdom of God. (used as a general concept for heaven) They may believe all one can do is to hope for the best. Besides, it is generally believed that all reasonably good people will be accepted. Whatever heaven or the next life holds, God is a good God. If He even exists? As long as one has faith and a general goodness, that is all that is required. To suggest there is a literal Hell to avoid and a heavenly paradise to gain, come on! That is a bit of an extreme position to hold. It is all speculation anyways. Nobody really knows, so they believe. We are a confused thinking people with no place to put our feet on solid ground. We are a people with no anchor of truth.

But is it wishful thinking that for the vast majority the door to heaven is very wide and generally open to all? Only the most deplorable and completely faithless will experience an heavenly denial. Can the majority really take comfort that those normal, and generally good people, can have peace that God is a loving and accepting God. He certainly will grant His Kingdom to those who are generally good. Even as the Pope now appears to be alluding too. That the atheists can even hold on to a hope that the door to heaven is open to them too, if the intent of their heart is good.

Regardless of what we prefer to believe, the question is still, is the Bible trustworthy and true? Was Christ telling the truth when He said that He was the only way to the Father? Remember the claim He made in the Gospel of John chapter 14, verse 6. The question is will we accept what He said? The fact is that He will never ever change. We treat our sin problem like a skin blemish and not as an eternal destiny issue. A concern we want emotional relief from so we feel better. But we are blind to the very words by Jesus Himself, that a refusal to make a decision based on the facts supporting the deity of Christ and His resurrection from the dead, will cause them for all eternity. The exclusivity of Him alone!

This is where the understanding of God Immutable holiness returns to the equation. If, as I alleged, God is unalterably holy, and due to His intrinsic nature, he cannot change, then the whole question is magnified. The expectations of most will be greatly misplaced. The inevitable will meet the reality of all of life. People do die, and are met with the situation that they are not prepared to meet God, not positionally holy. They have not met the perfect standards of pure righteousness. What a horrifying consequence! And, when this reality manifests itself to those trusting in alternative options, there will be no recourse. They will find that throughout all of eternity that God remains unalterably and immutable holy, and His justice is being satisfied. Either by personal accountability or because I am covered in the righteousness of Christ. There will be justice. The question is did I accept the complete satisfaction of that provided righteousness, because of what Christ did for me, or am I accepting the consequence of my own deficient merits, which will be shown to be absolutely inadequate. Both consequences last for all of eternity.

As I previously noted, I have long struggled with the thought of an eternal Hell, and so does most everyone I know who will spend any time considering its implications. It seems so unnatural and extreme. Unfair to the highest degree. It's like, really, Hell? An eternal and forever place of consequence. How can a loving God have such a place in His plan for mankind. A real destiny for those not covered in the righteousness of Christ. The only answer that is even somewhat conceivable, even remotely understandable, is when we return to the revelation of the immutable holiness, that is the intrinsic nature of God. He cannot tolerate, in His presence, sin to any degree, ever.

(Some reflections) As a person who made his living in law enforcement, I know there are consequences for illegal and immoral choices. The intent of the law is fairness. Blind justice. A consequence equal to the offense, and equally applied. Hell appears to be anything but fair! In my humanity, and as one who likes people, I want to push back against the whole concept. Because Hell appears to be an injustice in the highest degree! What kind of God would send someone to Hell? Let alone, one that is eternal in duration. While objectionable and hard to accept, it is logically understood only as one gets an vision of immutable holy! Not only intrinsically holy, but also immutably holy. So the point remains, at anypoint should God alter His standards, He would no longer be the revealed God of the scriptures. He would no longer be perfect. He would be like one of us, in the sense, He would be relatively good. His justice would be subjective. Yet, regardless of our desires to have a God we prefer, the nature of God is not subject to change. The litmus test remains. Sin unatoned for at death remains unatoned for all eternity.

I wish there was another way. I truly dislike this whole notion of an unchangeable God, who will never be other than He is, and therefore, cannot adjust His holy standards to suit my preferred standards. I do not get to make God in my own preferred image. It is God who is the creator. He made man in His image. When man does not measure up to that stated standard, the door is closed to having a relationship with Him. It will never alter! I need to be in a redeem, and new permanent relationship with God, one that is based on an acceptance that will never change. Since outside this perfect eternal standing, should I ever fall short of that infinite standard, the relationship would be rebroken. I would no longer be qualified. I need a permanent salvation. To compound the problem even more, I was born with a sin nature, so I am only doing what is according to my birth nature. So even if I could have avoided sin, I am not positionally holy. I need Christ's permanent righteousness credited to me. (Again, repeating these points by intent to emphasize the importance)

I fully understand why we dislike evangelism. I have mentioned repeatedly that it is disagreeable to me. It does not fit my preferred or natural personality. I am really an easy going and hopefully likable person. I am one of those guys who says hi to just about everyone. "Hey, how you doing", types. I like the environment that is portrayed on the old Andy

Griffith show. Sitting on the porch on Sunday afternoons and enjoying fellowship with those passing by our way. Folksy people who care for each other. Hanging out at the street curb, and chatting with our neighbors, as we inquire into their well-being and catching up on the family. Where most everyone is a decent person. I think you are getting the picture. This is a desired part of being human. The enjoyment of fellowship with our fellow man. Regardless of this preferred lifestyle, it does not nullify the truthfulness of what I previously wrote, there is an implied urgency to sharing the gospel. I know the uneasiness of the whole issue.

As I have noted a few times, my dislike of these subjects is so strong at times, I have even savored the idea of setting aside the whole kitten caboodle. Just turning off the idea of being a Christain, at least in the evangelical sense. I have entertained the idea more than once. Just get on living and forget the whole subject. Be a good guy and enjoy one's life.

However, to do that I must set aside those unavoidable questions that we all must face. Simply, what happens at death? Is there real truth? And, if I determine that the Christian faith is based on verifiable facts, can I just ignore them? I have my ticket to heaven verified and my destiny is secure. I could enjoy the fellowship of a local body of believers and engage in acts of kindness. That would give me a sense of purpose and may satisfy my need to be a positive difference maker. Helping people transverse through the journey of life with as little discomfort as possible. Helping people become whole and happy. I have considered more than once dropping out of the race. All because I do not enjoy the emotional discomfort of sharing my faith, and I like to be liked. But the implications and truthfulness of the faith do not allow that option. Therefore, to avoid the call of evangelism, I must set aside those issues of heaven and Hell, and the eternal destiny of those I love. And furthermore, this would result in my neglecting to influence the eternal destiny of the world that is available for me to impact. Is not the greatest love of all the willingness to self-sacrifice? Am I not willing to set aside my social discomfort, and standing in my community, if I really believe it is true? This is the tension! Between what I want from life and what I believe is ultimately true. What am I going to do with the question regarding the truthfulness of the Christian faith?

Be mindful, that we will be held responsible for our evangelistic efforts, or lack thereof. In the 20th chapter of Acts, Apostle Paul is recorded that he was free from the blood of all men since he did not hesitate to preach the gospel. Later in the book of 1st Corithians, in chapter 9, verse 16, he writes; woe is me if I do not preach the gospel. This is similar to the watchman in the book of Ezekiel. The failure to warn the unrepentant to change their ways, leaves the unrepentant responsible for their own sins. However, as in Ezekiel's warning, those who shrink back, are responsible for not warning them. This is not a heaven or hell question for the believer. But it is a warning for those of us who are responsible for sharing the faith. It is an accountability issue with the Lord. For the New Testament believer, it is likely that this accountability will be addressed at the Bema Seat of Christ, or by Fatherly discipline in this life. If we get caught up too much in this life, don't be surprised if God removes some of those cherished items from our lives. We are commanded to go and make disciples. That is even a step beyond evangelism. The question is did I love people enough knowing the eternal consequences? That I would set aside some of my desire to always be congenial to others, in order to share this hope that I have in Christ Jesus, even though it is uncomfortable? How can we claim Christianity is true if 95% of all professed believers never lead one person to saving faith? We become bolder in our faith, when we go from just believing, to counting it true in its full ramifications. I understand the dilemma. It is hard.

As you can see in this chapter, it was not so much about how to share our faith, but to understand the implications of our faith. Since few really enjoy the inherent responsibility that naturally comes with implications of the gospel. It can be very uncomfortable to even consider stepping out and engaging with others over their eternal destiny. Most people feel ill equipped to share, but there are some really good resources that can help. (Some really bad ones too) The idea of engaging in evangelism is a very unnatural feeling for most of us. So I wanted to recognize the stigma we all feel with the idea of evangelism. I was trying to capture the mental anguish we all grapple with over sharing our faith. That is why I was back and forth with the implications of the faith. Which is why the implication of being true is highlighted. It only makes sense because it is true, and life is so short. Ultimately, it is too eternally crucial to neglect, because it is true! If for this life only….. As the Apostle Paul wrote.

CHAPTER 15

Daily Christian living in light of eternity

Have you ever noticed while watching TV at night the themes of the commercials? In general, the theme is, you are not happy. How can you be happy if you are not driving our vehicle, eating our food, or drinking our beer. All of which they alleged will make you happy and popular. Or, if you drink and eat too much and you're overweight, you can be slender, sexually desirable, and happy, if you use our revolutionary and breakthrough diet or exercise program. The next major theme is; you are entitled to compensation. Someone must have harmed you, so allow us to sue them on your behalf. (To be sure, sometimes it is justified) But the general theme is you are not happy nor should you. You don't have what we are offering. This is far from the Biblical instruction to be satisfied with what the Lord has given us as our lot in life. Not that pursuing a better life is wrong, it just needs to be kept in perspective, with the mission we have been given.

We all desire the good life. We want the TV promises. We want our 2.5 kids. (I have never seen a half kid but you get my point) The house with a white fence on a cul de sac. The one with a big backyard and swimming pool. Add in an passionate sex life, a good standing in the community, financial success and we are well on our way to living the ideal television life. Should you achieve those goals you may well feel like you made it. But it is not real life, not in the real world's sense. Maybe that's why so many are so unhappy. There is the illusion and then there is real life. And real life seldom measures up to the illusion. We have more than the majority of the world, and yet, we are among the most unhappy. Many places are horrible places to be Christian. Serious persecution is taking place all over the world. There are vast numbers of Christians suffering unbelievable persecution. My own life is quite comfortable to be honest. It is my "natural" desire to keep it that way. The reality is, there are hard aspects of living in this fallen world. Life can be very hard and heartbreaking.

Maybe as I age, my fantasy is the desire to go back to simple life as a younger adult, with insignificant issues. Those fond memories of my simpler days. Maybe that's why I still enjoy the old 1960's family shows. We all know that this was not real life, but certainly a life that appeals to me. A simple life with little problems and real community. No big eternal question to wrestle with. Turn it off and enjoy a life of friends, family and community interest. They even incorporated the church into their lives. They just don't take it too seriously. It was a religious discipline that helped them be better and more rounded people. The practice created a better community but no heaven or hell issues to consider. It was generally an expectation to attend church. Unfortunately, this is not real life, sadly not! I really do think I would enjoy my life more if I did turn it all off. It is my personality.

Obviously, life can be burdensome. It is also obvious that life is very very hard for many people. Many live ominously without much purpose. Just living day to day. Making the best of it while waiting to die. Seems a bit defeatist but practically true for many. This is why so many televangelists are finding a harvest from the bank accounts of the deceived faithful. They promise you the illusion that your life could be like their life, if you have enough faith, and give enough money to their ministry. If you just make that "faith promise", then you will have the life they are enjoying. I have a suggestion. Why not try that same principle in reverse. If it is a real principle? Give money to the struggling and see if those alleged promised prosperities come back to the ministry. If I offended anyone? So what! People are struggling and to solicit money for your luxury is wrong. To live in luxury at the expense of others, while the less fortunate live meger lives, is unbiblical. Stop twisting scriptures! There is a saying, that for the believer this is the only Hell we will face, for the unbeliever, this is the only heaven. This is not consistent with the illusion being promised by those spiritual materialists. (Sorry, I got off track again with soupbox commentary)

So much of what we do is essentially meaningless, yet we pursue them with passion. Think of golf. I like golf, but when one thinks of the object of the game it becomes kinda silly. A golfer will hit a ball down the fairway, only to hit it again, until the objective is achieved, the ball goes into a hole. Golf is not a particularly meaningful activity. I find it is a good place to have some fellowship, as I have enjoyed many rounds of golf with close friends, family and my dear wife. But never has it changed my life or affected eternity. There are good secondary reasons to enrich life via shared common interest, but these activities should never be life defining in themselves. A distraction for a while to amuse ourselves. Simple pleasures, of which I have enjoyed over the years. So I am not suggesting for a moment not to engage, because if I did, I would be a hypocrite, since I enjoy those activities.

Furthermore, these activities can enhance the quality of life and give diversity to individual experiences. We should enjoy those gifts from the hand of God. Since one size fits all would make life bland. A mind that is totally focused on the serious would be unsustainable. We all need reprieves from the stresses of life. We all need to take time to laugh and enjoy the goodness of life. I have benefited from the mutual interest with others. I have long enjoyed sports, a good laugh, and other divergent interests. I like the camaraderie and unity of teamwork that are part of sports. Men or women from different backgrounds working together for the common goal. One of my particular interests is being a fan of the Detroit Lions. Unfortunately, after many Sunday afternoons watching a game, I find myself a bit disillusioned that I wasted the afternoon in futility. There needs to be a proper perspective that makes these pursuits meaningful and also enriching, but not life defining. (The book of Ecclesiastes)

Many of these activities are opportunities to develop lasting friendships. It is the unbalanced interest in these activities that will eventually draw one away from the pursuit of those greater responsibilities, like those of family, marriage and ministry. When we become overly engaged we lose the benefits. Many individuals, after years of pursuing financial success, hobbies, or any other pursuits of interest, find that these pursuits of pleasure are fleeting. If we define our worth by the win we will be disillusioned. I understand the objective in sports is winning. That is the nature of playing the game. However, regardless of how good you become, there will always be someone who will surpass our achievements. Even at the top, the time there is temporary, there will soon be someone who does it better. We chase and chase and chase only to grasp the air of meaninglessness. Once again, like those reflections of Soloman in the book of Ecclesiastes. He pursued everything that could be perceived to bring meaning to life, only to reflect that in the end that it was all vanity. He reflects at the end of the book that for life to have real meaning, it needs a God focused perspective, to give life real meaning. Solomon writes a number of times that we are to enjoy the simple pleasures God gives. So enjoy! But keep in balance and perspective.

Likely why so many struggle in midlife crisis. They feel the more fruitful days are slipping away. This results in a desire to recapture what is left of those passing years. This happens when our minds are not focused on the promises of a life that is beyond description, and the purpose for which God created us. If we lose our way, we may try to grasp in foolish desperation, what is remaining of this fleeting life, thereby, messing up a lifetime of investment in our personal relationships. We have all known the man or woman who became dissatisfied with their lot in life, because of the deceptive illusion portrayed by TV or movies, and made the foolish decision to pursue greener pastures. Feeling like they missed out on something they deserved, or is missing from their lives, that will make them feel rejuvenated. It is a deceiving illusion. Sometimes the grass appears greener on the other side of the fence because the field is full of manure. (I thought of another word but wanted to be Christ-like) Step on the other side of the fence and see what our feet have stepped into. The false promises of a better life, but many will pursue it anyway, regardless of the consequences. That is how strong our fleshly and selfish nature can be at times, some want the illusion, even though it is an illusion.

At least what they hoped would bring renewed meaning to the fleeting years of their lives, renewed sexual satisfaction, or freedom from the daily grind. In the process, they hurt many loved ones in their lives, particularly the spouse to whom they made a covenant promise. And their children! The very ones they would have died for if needed. Now, by chasing what they feel are unmet needs, they abandon most everything that has real lasting meaning. They leave for a bit of temporary satisfaction at the well of illusion, thereby, complicating everything in their lives. I am going to be a bit graphic here with the men. I have long enjoyed my sex life with my wife, but a boob is a boob, and even with a new boob, will become the same boob in time. We need to keep in focus, that life grows richer in meaning, as we grow together through the journey of life. It is the richness of the relationship that makes the intimate life sacred, and meaningful between a man and his wife. The enduring journey through many of the trials of life. The shared engagement of raising a family with a forever partner. The journey that leaves the type of lasting memories we want to leave. A real legacy of honor that our children will admire.

(My warning) So avoid the damage of everything you have worked hard for and nurture your present marriage. There are ways to keep your sex life meaningful at home. It is a reflection on the quality of marriage that God intended for us, and a witness to an unbelieving world. Furthermore, the investment in your marriage is an investment in your testimony, and your children's admiration of you. Even as adult children, the stability of their parent's marriage gives stability to their own lives. The steady anchor for the whole family. It shows to their families, and the watching world, that there are God defining relationships, that are worthy of honoring as a commitment for lifetime. Sadly lacking in today's world. Let's continue.

There is something that is honorable to a lasting legacy. One that preserved through the struggles of life. A life, upon passing, leaves fond memories and the lasting impact into the lives of those left behind. Principled living. It is hard in today's world. There are far more temptations in today's world. The community standards are changing fast. Sex is promoted, in our faces, and then people are shocked when temptation befalls another believer. Keeping pure eyes is hard. Try to find a decent movie that does not over promote sex. Even on evening TV, I am seeing old 1950 Playboy standards, as common on prime time. Even a female razor commercial that is a bit too graphic. What was once considered erotic in its day, is now the norm. This is the lure of today's world.

The danger is that we become enchanted with the world and pursue the greener pastures. We throw off moral restraints and pursue the lure of temptation. Which only leaves regret and pain. In the process we damage our testimonies, thereby, forgoing the chance to be difference makers.

Be sure we will all stand before God as believers and give an account on how we lived out our Christian lives. We are eternally saved but still accountable. How we live does matter. The temptations may be great, but endurance is worthy of your commitment. If we do not keep a check on ourselves the results will be regrettable. We may find temporal pleasure, but as most experience, great regret.

You may find this a bit humorous, but I can remember playing Monopoly as a youngster, and saying Connecticut cut cut your butt and thought it was a bit naughty. The world has changed. The church and individual believers have too. I can remember years ago when we joined a church, there were expectations that you would not attend movies or even dance with your wife in public. (To clarify, I like movies and will dance with my wife) I think some of those expectations were artificial legalism masquerading as real internal righteousness. Then again, maybe good old fashioned wisdom, that protected us from sinful compromise. I have a dear neighbor who wears a dress while working in the yard. I have great admiration for her wholesomeness. A Godly lady. Not my standards of attire for work in the yard, but admirable just the same. Just contrasting how rapidly the world has changed.

This is why this reflection of the holy and the temporariness of life is needed. It needs to be refocused in today's day and age. It needs to be a higher pursued standard in my own life. The changing culture has impacted the church. We also normalized the world's values into our personal lives. Adapting the values, and over time, accepting them as normal. It is affecting our message, our communities, and our personal lives. Those worldly values have practical effects on every aspect of our society and personal lives. That consciousness of the holy is evaporating from our churches. The drift of compromise from Biblical based truth has lessened the urgent call for faith sharing. We once understood the eternal repercussions of choices. Now our concern for those outside the faith is seldom heard from the pulpit. We lost our zeal to share the hope in the gospel. Without the mindset of holy, everything seems okay. If we falsely perceive that we are okay in ourselves, we will not see a need for the hope of the gospel. Everything is interconnected ultimately to God's immutable holy nature. The litmus test previously given.

The growing compromise affects the practical aspects of our Christian faith too. Our Heavenly Father desires us to be models of the inherent goodness of our Savior, for which we will be accountable one day. For the compromising believer, loss of blessings, prayers that go unanswered, accountability at the Bema Seat of Christ and/or divine discipline in this life. As we lose the understanding of immutable holy, we lose the appreciation of our indescribable salvation. We may even abandon the truth since we can no longer accept the implications of our faith being true. Satan is having a field day. That is why he is so desiring to have the saints fail. The ruining of a testimony stalls our ability to be a witness. When we compromise with the world to fit in, we have little to offer, but soup kitchens. Full stomachs and eternally lost souls.

When we grasp the eternal perspective it changes our motivations. We see that choices have consequences, eternal ones. When we understand that God is not going to change His standards we quit secret sins. When we understand the tremendous gift we have in our eternal salvation, we start to distance ourselves from the temporariness of this life, and look more desirably at the life to come. Our incomprehensible salvation becomes our greatest source of joy. One would think that as we age we would be more cognitive of the inescapability of death. Thereby more diligently focused on eternal things. But that is not being manifested in many lives I know. They too have been caught by the changing culture. It has negatively impacted their spiritual growth and priorities. They are not finishing fruitfully. They are adapting to the culture. They have allowed CNN to be their standard for truth and not the Bible. It is time to reassess our temporal life and recall our legacy we are leaving behind. Will we have a lasting spiritual impact or pursue temporary pleasures?

What determines if a life is worth living through these tribulations and difficulties? It is when it is lived, as an anchored life, for the purposes of God, knowing that our faithfulness will be rewarded. But not until the Bema Seat will each of us know the full impact of our lives.

CHAPTER 16

Christian living and our prayer life

There is an area of my life that is regularly lacking, my prayer life. It does not make sense! I DO believe God answers prayer. Somehow TV gets more of my free time than it should. Not much life changing has ever happened watching TV. Generally, it is a waste of time, and wasted money on an expensive cable bill. Which is ironic, since one of the unsettling thoughts I wrestle with, is the passing of time. The inability to recapture time that has passed. Because time once lost is now lost forever. So I need to remind myself to make prayer a priority in my personal life. To set before the Lord, those priorities of what I am concerned about. Particularly, that the eyes of unbelievers of whom I want to witness, would be opened to spiritual matters. Praying that they would understand the holiness of God, their need for salvation, and accept the offer of the free gift of life, eternal life. That offer is limited to time, and once passed, is lost forever. Furthermore, I need to be mindful that even in my prayer life, and yours too, holiness is an issue. I cannot walk in willful disobedience and expect God's blessing. No powerful movement of God can take place in the lives of the disobedient, nor for those who are not engaged in active praying.

Yet praying often feels like a frustrating endeavor. To be honest, I have often felt "it appears" at times to be a fruitless experience. I have friends who have regular and effective prayer lives, not so much for me. Sometimes it feels like a waste of time, because I have prayed for many things in my life, with little to no evidence to show. I feel like asking God, and I have, what is the use. I know God is able, but when for no understandable reason, He just does not appear to show up, I get frustrated and want to give up what I perceive is a waste of time. And as often is the case, I find the TV an appealing way to waste time. And yet if you were to ask me, I would confess that I believe prayer moves the hand of God, a bit illogical don't you think.

Now the reasons are innumerable as to why God operates in certain ways. For me, shall I say, many are still unrecognizable. But here some are basic principles of having prayers answered. (you can do additional research if you desire greater knowledge) The Bible says if I harbor sin in my heart, God will not answer. (Psalms 66:18) Alternatively, it says that the prayers of a righteous man are powerful and effective. (James 5:16b) No doubt that there are areas in my life that are lacking. Areas that need spiritual growth. Perhaps, God is waiting for me to pursue holy living with greater diligence. I also know there is a warning to husbands, that if they do not treat their wives with proper care and love, He will not listen. Be clear, He is not saying that they are not born again. He is stating a principle for His children on how to have intimacy with Him, which results in more favorable responses to our prayers. I am thankful that my wife and I have a quality marriage. I give most credit to her. She is one of the finest people I know. A wonderful mother and grandmother. Nana to the grandkids. A faithful partner! The point is, God is indicating there are conditions to having our prayers answered. One cannot live like the devil and expect prayers to be answered like they are living saintly.

He is also sovereignly working out a plan that I may not see or understand. I understand that there is a bit of a mystery between the sovereignty of God and the free will of man. Depending on individual theological perspective, Christians will drift usually toward one of the two. Some go so far as to say that God cannot act unless they are the initiators. Others believe God is going to do what He is going to do, so why even bother. I try to take a balanced Biblical perspective, since the Bible teaches both. And truth be told, I don't have this locked down, nor does anyone completely. Those who claim they do can be quickly exposed with a few pointed questions. There is a bit of enigma when it comes to how and why God acts as He does.

When we try to understand the ways of God we will quickly find ourselves in very deep water. In general, I believe the Bible describes both as being true, how that can be, I don't fully understand. Yet, when

I ponder it, it is clear to me that both must be true! If we are truly going to be responsible, I must be at least somewhat free to choose. However, unless God is sovereign over history, no prophecy could ever be assured. Yet, God had declared the beginning to the end, human history. And, when He commands, there is the assumption that I can obey, at least to some degree. Therefore, when he commands, I am being held responsible, even if it is beyond my full ability. He has said to be holy since He is holy. Now I can be better, and walk according to the Spirit which will reveal a more holy life, but I will never be holy in an absolute sense. Since He has revealed aspects of both, we should endeavor to understand both Biblical principles. One perspective shows our personal responsibilities and the other gives assurance that God is still in ultimate control.

Nonetheless, there are human limitations to understanding these subjects. The finite can never grasp the infinite. Understanding the ways God will always be beyond full human comprehension. We can grow in our comprehension of these revelations but there is a limit to our human understanding. This is true of prayer also. When and how God chooses to respond is often beyond our understanding. I know it can be frustrating at times. There are many, beyond our knowledge, reasons why God is doing what He is doing. (Just read the book of Job) This is where the walk of faith comes in. Walking and trusting even when I do not know what is going on beyond my, or your ability to perceive.

As an example, I may pray and not understand spiritual warfare in the heavenlies, or the sovereign plans of God. This I know, I am instructed to pray. To pray that the eyes of the unbelievers would be open so they can see the hope of the gospel. To pray for physical and emotional healing, and for struggling marriages. To pray for open doors so I can naturally share my faith. Nonetheless, I must also understand that God has given us, and those we pray for free will. I must allow God to be God in all things, even when I don't understand. So when I cannot think of any reasonable reason why a particular prayer should not be answered in the manner that I believe it should, I need to rest in the sovereign reasons of an Almighty God. For this life is temporary and answers may only be understood in eternity.

So if you have troubles with prayer as I do? Review reasons why your prayers may not be answered. Is there known sin in your life? Are we mindful that we are wrestling in spiritual warfare? Are we remembering that those we are praying for still have free will? Is my prayer in line with His will? Am I allowing God to be the sovereign God even if I don't understand His ways? Oftentimes, it is likely we have different timetables or ultimate purposes. These are principles that I need to incorporate better in my own life. Maybe that's why I am writing this short chapter. Maybe it's not for you, but a reminder for me! To refresh in my mind the importance of prayer and also some of the principles of prayer. Even if I am wrestling with some confusion over the results.

I should emphasize once more, if there are a few areas that should be a regular focus, it would be for the salvation of others, because Satan has blinded the eyes of unbelievers. (2nd Corinthians 4:4) This is one of the means for which God has sovereignly designed for us to impact the world. Certainly, we who have children, want first and foremost, the individual salvation of our offspring. Lastly, our prayers should also include a prayer for the movement of God in our time. We certainly need it! Since God has in His sovereign wisdom placed us in this time and place of history for a reason, He expects us to be difference makers where we are placed. Much of this will not happen if it is not soaked in prayer. A discipline that I need to work on. A faithfulness, that all who engage in, will be rewarded for at the Bema Seat of Christ.

CHAPTER 17

The personal consequences of living in a fallen world and the hope of the Gospel

Is it sacreligious to say there are times I don't enjoy being a Christian? I do not even like to be good sometimes. I believe I am generally a good person. But there are times when it is wearing trying to live up to those standards that we envisioned from a Christian, not in order to be saved, but a reasonable service unto the Lord. In light of God's mercy, it is a reasonable service to sacrifice some of my temporal comforts for the advancement of the Eternal Kingdom. Actually, it would be reasonable to sacrifice all temporal pleasures, in light of eternity. This was the Apostle Paul's perspective. He gave up his high standing in the Jewish community, and privileged authority, to pursue the greater goals God had for him. (See Phillippians chapter 3) The same appreciation of what we now possess, our tremendous gift of eternal salvation, should produce a similar mindset. This would indicate by our actions, that we have a solid comprehension of what we truly have been given, an eternal redeemed life. This is the expected life for all Christians. (Once again to be absolutely clear that moral change is a desired expectation but not a condition of our salvation. I agree with the Chafer Theological Seminary statement in the section on Soteriology. One can find the doctrine statement on their website) These expectations come as part of my identity as a Christian, for a watching world. Those who often evaluate the merits of Christainity based on the authenticity of the Christian's walk. And for this to be realized, requires a Christian to pursue a lifestyle of consistent righteous living, even though it can seem out of touch with the world we live in.

Likely one of the reasons why I preferred jail ministry. There is very little stigma with the inmates with whom I minister. The incarcerated, those who knew I worked there, gave me some instant credibility. If an officer in uniform is willing to humble himself enough to return to the jail at night to share the gospel, then maybe he is worth giving a hearing. Since it is purely a volunteer activity on my part, it showed that I truly care. It is, in another sense of the word, a captive audience who often have nothing else to do. (Sorry, it is the reality of the situation) I know there are many that I work with who see my ministry as fraternizing with the enemy. The validation of the bad guys. To be sure, jails house some of society's most immoral men and women, people we need to be protected from. The pod I taught in was maximum security. Many whom are sex offenders. Others are incarcerated for murder or other serious crimes. Not exactly the prime of society when it comes to high moral standards, but created by God just the same. Therefore, they have worth in the eyes of God. As with all sin, it is just a matter of degrees. In light of God's immutable holiness we all fall short of the Glory of God. Infinity short! Think of this way, if I am on the side of the rising sun, and you are on the other side of me, I can say I am closer to the sun than you, but we are both roughly 93 million miles from the sun.

I tend to think of it another way when it comes to ministry in the jail-there by the grace of God goes I. I was fortunate to be raised in a quasi Christian family. Had I been born into another family or neighborhood, my outcome likely would have been different. My inherent sinfulness likely would have led my life in another direction. Oftentimes it is largely dependent on the deck of cards we are dealt. Those that we had no choice in. I did not choose my parents or the neighborhood I grew up in. This is why some compassion should be afforded when it comes to those less fortunate in life. Not everyone had the same favorable cards. Had the deck of cards been different, any of us could have found ourselves manifesting the same outcome. Sin can become a master of anyone of us. The degree of sin is often just the opportunity to express itself in an individual's lives. The degree of supporting restraint is often the difference. I recognized that

I was fortunate, therefore, compassionate. This is not to say that many don't agitate me with their nonsense and ongoing deviant behavior. Let's continue to explore this issue.

Those incarcerated often come from drug infused neighborhoods. They generally lack a Godly heritage. Most have educational or mental health issues. The moral decay in some of the neighborhoods where they grew up is rampant. It is my strong conviction that the number one issue resulting in deviant behavior, is a lack of Godly men in their homes. Men who should be expected to lead their children in the ways of life. Installing the heritage of principle living. Simply stated; many men are not being responsible in their God given duties. They are failing to be a strong presence in the home, with the desired purpose of raising their sons and/or daughters into responsible adulthood. And this brokenness of the family has been accelerated by women who have lost their perception of moral wholesomeness. It is clear that way too many children are born outside the God ordained design for the family. Sexual morality is not a result of economic status, since the ability to say no is not conditioned on resources, but the consequence of that morality does affect their economic status. Numerous sociological studies have shown these statements to be true. Just do a quick web search to validate the truthfulness of this statement. I personally see it via my work history.

I, as have many others, have noted the societal and personal grounding benefits of those moral practices that are derived from the teachings of the Bible. Values like honesty, commitment to marriage, hard work, sexual restraint, and personal responsibility are all good foundations for every society. I even wrote a research paper to that effect in a psychology class at a secular college. To the credit of the professor it was well received. It was my contention that basic Biblical principles provided stabilizing benefits to those individuals who practice the faith. Which inturn promotes a positive mental health effect. It also creates stronger families, safer and healthier neighborhoods. It is clear that nurturing those aspects of our spiritual nature generally results in being a better citizen.

That is why it is troubling when many of our leaders think those influences of Biblical principles should be removed. They maintain that we cannot have Christianity taught in our public schools. An endorsement of a particular religion they say. But all morality must have an understructure.

Some standard of truth. They fail to see that removal of Christian morality is unstabilizing for society. That the removal of our foundational moral principles, that reverberate from our faith, is not good for society. There is a strong correlation between those virtuous Christian teachings and strong neighborhoods and communities. When we replace our moral foundations with Godless principles, we have no standard. Godless morality is no morality.

This is manifested in the growing educational push to be free from all religious principles. Think this through, since it really is quite simple, when the dignity of humanity is reduced to that of a later stage of the evolutionary process, it is hard to expect people to see why they should adhere to ethical standards. If all we are is a higher developed animal, then why should we be surprised if some act according to this alleged nature. Animals are animals no matter how well we dress up their image. If that is the conclusion? It is hard to impress on those receiving this teaching that life has real meaning. It is the truth that we are created in the very image of God, that will truly give a sense of intrinsic worth. This has played out in many people's lives. Read the Jeffrey Dahmer story. He placed a good part of the blame for his moral choices, on the devaluing of life, via the teaching of evolution. If all we are is an animal, then why can we not be eaten? He thought so! Crazy world we are living in. What we promote as ideas does have practical ramifications. What foundation we build upon is crucial. Ideas have consequences. Hitler had ideas of morality. So did Dietrich Bonhoeffer. They were a world apart.

I have noted it a number of times in conversations, and I am not sure if the idea was an originated idea, or the thoughts came from another. That even if I knew Christianity was unsupported by any credible evidence, I would still want it taught in schools and emphasized in our communities. I contend that we cannot have a healthy nation if the moral foundations are removed. Even if our faith was without merit, there are still solid practical benefits, to advocate it as a good moral foundation for a society. That is a simple truth. (Psalms 11:3) Therefore, while the benefits are the byproduct of these principles, all foundational truth needs to be anchored on something that is always true, and that is the immutable nature of God. So it is ultimately God's intrinsic nature that is the basis for those values that make our lives grounded and healthy. (And to be absolutely clear, Christianity is founded on very sound evidence)

Those who are extracting the Christian faith from our societies are seeing the fruit of their actions. The brokenness becomes more obvious everyday. We can see we are slowly destroying ourselves with unrestrained moral freedom. This is obvious in the lives of those who are housed in the prisons and jails. This tolerance of deviance is being advanced to the rest of us as the new sacred value. It is now considered noble to be tolerant of most everything, and considered to be intolerant if we hold to an expectation of personal responsibility. The foundations we build on have consequences. This is why we need the message of truth and Grace. First in prevention and then the second in redemption.

Let's explore this in practical real life. (While I don't teach in a womens pod) Where is the hope for someone who has engaged in the drug culture? The type of lifestyle that often leads to very promiscuous living. How does one recover from the emotional stains of prostitution? After years of degrading yourself for drugs, which often then leads to more promiscuous living, how is one to find hope? How does one restore a sense of wholeness, after years of sexual degradation? What can a secular counselor do to help rebuild a life after being morally compromised by promiscuous living? You can analized forever the root causes. Offer some practical advice for positive change. But such counseling does not lead to a renewed sense of wholeness. That can come only through the gospel of Jesus Christ, which is able to restore a person to a renewed life. And Jesus is the master of restoring lives. It was His model of ministry, validating the worth of a person, regardless of their past. And only the gospel of Jesus Christ results in this becoming a reality. Furthermore, when we abandon truth, we abandon our anchor for being moral. For when we abandon truth we abandon the Gospel. Because the gospel is the truth of God's redeeming love.

This is the uniqueness of the gospel. Many religions teach some form of moral living. Only the gospel gives new life. While it is true that sin is present in all of our lives, and we all have regrets, to one degree or another. There are some sins involving sexual behavior, or those actions that have hurt another, that particularly linger in one's soul with a sense of regret, shame, and remorse. These unchangeable actions are some of the most difficult to overcome emotionally. It may appear to those so scared by these lifestyles, that the ability to restore a state of wholeness, is impossible. They therefore abandon the effort to even try. They lose their desire, because the hope of ever arriving at a state of respectability, appears to be unattainable. However, when they see that their worth is determined, not by personal choices, but by the God who validates them and extends His love, they may find that all hope is not lost. It all starts with the renewing hope of God's redeeming grace.

It has been said that the value of something is the price that is paid for something. In this case, the value of a soul is of tremendous value, since God the Father paid for your soul with the blood of Christ. Therefore, you must possess profound worth. This, then, becomes our hope. The knowledge that God sees us as immensely valuable even in our sin, since Christ died for us even as sinners. If we are loved as sinners, think how much more as His children. (Romans chapter 5:8-9)) Then for those who do respond to the gospel, the understanding that they have become clothed in the very righteousness of Christ, is the impetus to growth in the Christian life. This with the desired goal of showing that transformation, because to the outside world, the inward transformation is unseen, unless the newly redeemed manifest it to the world in which they live. The world cannot see the spiritual new birth. They cannot see something life changing has taken place in one's life. Therefore, the newly redeemed need to take practical sanctification steps to show the world that something has changed in their lives, if they want their conversion to be taken seriously by others! Since the evidence of the life changing hope of the gospel has been received, can only be noticed by others, by a changed life. This necessitates some real sanctification in their lives, even though they are fully accepted as a child of God, at the very moment they accept the gospel of eternal life. But if you want others to believe a change has really happened? Then one needs to manifest it to the world, by showing a newness of Christ-like behavior. Otherwise others will see only the shell of the new you. We who have been redeemed should no longer live according to our old nature, that is not God's desire for any of His children. A new life should show a new lifestyle, even though we are fully accepted at the very moment of our salvation. Without works!

This is the hope that comes only in the Christian message. The gospel of Jesus Christ. The hope that starts with the understanding of God's redeeming love. This is the most crucial starting point. The discernment that in God's eyes, they still have indelible value. To become aware that God is a God of new beginnings. The felt need is the desire for authentic love. This is often the first step in that redemptive process. This is the reason many first come to faith, for the emotional unmet love needs. While this may be the drawing reason, the greatest benefit is the forgiveness of sin and eternal life, but that may not be the original draw. Everyone one has a natural desire to be authentically and unconditionally loved.

For us who are redeemed, the best place to start in reaching out to those lost and deeply hurt in the despair of life, is by sharing this vision of hope. Which is the love of God being portrayed in the cross of Christ. Because those feelings of unworthiness are almost unbearable, resulting in a sense of despair, since they perceive no hope. Therefore, without this hope, they continue in those ever increasing destructive lifestyles, joining those in similar lifestyles. There is acceptance with those who too have found themselves in the despair of life. Those sharing the feeling of being unworthy of true love. It lessens the stigma of those regrettable choices. It is a world of lost hope. And to protect their fragile wounded souls, they often put up a very hard outer crude image, as though they are not troubled by their lifestyles. But the pain is real and very deep in their souls. This is why redemption in the gospel is so freeing. But it is also so hard to fully believe and accept. It is hard to grasp that no one is beyond the love of God. While He knows everything about everything, He still loves the unlovable. Just read in the gospels how Jesus interacted with the lowly of society. The unlovable, at least in how they perceive themselves in their own eyes, and most often in the eyes of society. Those who have been scarred by the devaluing effects of sexual sin.

Regardless of the reality of this hope, remember that the true love of God is often hard to convey to the one so devastated by a life of sin. There is often a long progression of drug use that leads to a lifestyle of regretable sexual sin. Or, it can start with sexual sin, that leads to drug use to mask the pain. While in either case, they have a deep desire to experience this love, it is an unknown love. They have a most difficult time accepting this pure love, as unconditionally expressed in the gospel. Oftentimes because of the way Christians have treated them or lived hypocritical lives. These devaluing feelings also may come to the person who is the victim of sexual abuse. Which is no fault of their own. Which then leads to the feeling of unworthiness. Which then leads to other self-deprecating actions, that compounds the feelings of unworthiness. A vicious vicious cycle. The feeling of being purely loved is hard to accept. Those caught up in the cycle of sin do not know what authentic love is, so they often settle for being used love.

So how is the cycle broken? It starts with the genuine love of Christ. When one grasps the hope that they can start afresh, with a brand new identity we can find in Christ, the first glimmers of hope are realized. They are already fully aware of their sinfulness, no matter how much they portray a sense of denial. What they have a hard time grasping is that God still has arms open to those so willing. A chance to start again with a new identity as a child of the living God. No longer living with the identity of a prostitute, or their history of being sexual permissive, or that as a criminal, but that of a child of the King. The first step comes by the simple comprehension of God's desire to accept them into His family. The desire of God to every member of the human race is that they too can be accepted as a full member in the body of Christ. Fully adopted and fully accepted! But it must start where it started with each of us, the choice to accept God's love offer. When this is understood and accepted, the practical sanctification aspects of redemption should start. Then the freedom and renewed wholesomeness develops as they come to know, and then grow in that knowledge of their new identity. Their new creation in Christ starts to be manifested with new practical aspects of a restored life. A witness to the world of the redemptive love of Christ. They become a walking testimony of the goodness of God's grace.

This is something that no secular counseling can offer, nor the criminal justice system. Not just the changing of their eternal destination by the acceptance of the gift of eternal life, but by joining the family of God, they change forever who they are in identity. The prospect to begin again is life affirming to the one who will accept this love. The knowledge of having been clothed in the very righteousness of Christ, adopted and accepted in Christ, is freeing. This again, is where the wisdom given to the Apostle Paul comes again into the equation. In Philippians, chapter 3, he writes the one thing he did was putting the past behind him, and striving for the goal in Christ. (my loose paraphrase) What great wisdom from a man who once persecuted the church of the living God. Should Paul have stayed in that regretful time in his life, his ministry would never have shown the fruit that it did. He would have stayed stuck in regret and guilt. Not God's desired plan for any of us.

There is an offer from God that is beyond anything this secular world could ever offer. The chance to be fully forgiven. The putting on the righteousness of Christ. Being able to rejoice in the fact that they have been adopted and born anew into the family of the Almighty God of our souls. What a wonderful promise and offer! What an opportunity for a new beginning. An opportunity that is offered to those so deeply wounded by the scars of life. A completely new identity, and beginning. A chance to put the emotional scars of sin, and a life of poor choices behind them, and now be seen as a child of the living God! A new creation in Christ. Then they can look forward to the day when this old fleshly nature is totally gone and they celebrate their glorification in heaven. Hallelujah what a Savior!

Our call of responsibility

This will only happen for those so devastated by the scars of life when we as the body of Christ undertake the responsibility to share this hope. The renewing hope contained in the gospel of Jesus Christ. This message needs to continue in discipleship. The learning of their new identity needs to be developed and explained. This motivation to share this hope comes when the believer understands the consequences, both temporarily and eternally. When we undertake the ministry to express authentic love. And we undertake that responsibility seriously. No doubt we are called to be the messengers of hope to a dying world. Only Christianity has the ultimate message of hope. Why are we keeping this message of hope to ourselves? The scriptures instruct us to be ambassadors of the hope of the gospel. We who are redeemed need to be messengers of the way to redemption. Because those so scared by sin, need to know how wide and long and high and deep is the love of God. (Ephesians 3:18) Because the acceptance of pure love is very hard to grasp after being so deep in the grip of sin. For those who have been betrayed and/or violated by the actions of others, which later led to their own contribution to this despair, it is the stigma of shame that is almost impossible to overcome. It is the qualifications of Jesus Christ as the God/man, and the completeness of the work of Jesus Christ on the cross, that gives this ambition to move past the past, and begin again. We Christians who have been redeemed, now have the responsibility to be messengers of the way to redemption.

I am in no way suggesting that the God ordained role of government be set aside. We need protection and upheld accountability of individual actions. I am saying that there are two different focusses. There is the role of the government to protect us. And then the role of Christians being ambassadors of Christ, for the purpose of sharing the way to a redeemed life. These two functions are part of God's plan. One is the safety of our society. The other is the life changing message of salvation and redemption. Which is another way of saying less crime. (Our world is full of broken people that result from the devastating effects of sin) Furthermore, once those who have entered into the criminal justice system or rehabs, the real hope for the restoration of their lives. Which is another way of saying less crime, and less self-deprecating choices in the future by many of these offenders.

(My editorial) The removal of the moral foundations by our media, entertainment industry and our governments results in self-destructive outcomes. Broken and devastated lives are the byproducts of this movement. The government and the entertainment industry now promote lifestyles that are self-destructive to our society. And then requests almost unlimited resources to help those devalued by these actions. But these resources that they offer are futile for the changing of lives. The very efforts to promote freedom that is not grounded in Biblical morality only leads to wounded souls. Lastly, the body of Christ does not help the situation, if we abandon our message or our values. We need stable and wholesome foundations or we will unravel. Not too hard to understand is it?

CHAPTER 18

Legalism or Discipleship

There is nothing so frustrating in the Christian's walk as trying to merit our Heavenly Father's love. He is love! It is another key aspect of His essence. When we have become His children, we are accepted in His beloved, that is Christ Jesus. That is what is meant by being in Christ. Once the payment for our sins, which has been already accomplished on the cross by Christ Jesus, and then accepted by a sinner as full payment of their sins, God the Father is free to express His love. His just demands are satisfied. His wrath on sin has been propitiate. Which means, He is forever satisfied with Christ's payment, for those who have believed in Christ Jesus.

This has been an area of theology that took me some time to appreciate. It took years to absorb the significance of this vital teaching of the scriptures. The understanding that my relationship with God was forever settled. I am His! Now and forever! This is another occasion where we need to stop and allow this aspect of the gospel truth to anchor into our souls. We read through pivotal teachings only to quickly move on to the next point, without allowing freeing truths to sink deeply into our souls. These are some of the tremendous blessings our Heavenly Father wants us to know and celebrate. God, our Abba Father, wants us to know that we who are in Christ, that we understand we are eternally His. (See 1st John chapter 5, along with numerous other sections of the scriptures) We have been purchased by the blood of Christ. The knowledge of our permanent sonship/daughtership, is one of the key elements of our freely given salvation that needs to be known and celebrated. (Also see Ephesians, particularly the 1st chapter) Freely given according to His grace. And, Grace by definition, is unmerited. For me, it was crucial to understand this aspect of our salvation, in order to experience the assurance of my eternal destiny. It relieved me of the anguish of conditional salvation teachings. And this confidence continues to grow, as I realize the significance of this Biblical truth. This growing insight into sound theology is grounding and freeing. As Jesus said, you shall know the truth, and that truth will set you free. (John 8:32) (My paraphrase based on numerous translations) To be free, depends on knowing the truth, once a son is always a son, and that is a liberating truth.

This leads to another facet of theological teachings that needs to be explored, and understood, to give clarity to the subject. The themes of Justification and Sanctification. If we confuse these, we will be subject to uncertainty in regards to certain aspects of our salvation. This topic can be a bit complex when we start to look at these teachings in their different applications. So I am going to keep the subject matter, as generally understood, in its primary application. Justification has to do with my standing before God. To be right with God requires 100% perfect righteousness. In order to qualify for heaven, I need to be positionally perfect. This is justification. It is a legal declaration from God about every believer in Christ. I am seen as perfectly righteous. A judicial declaration by the Judge of the universe. (Romans 8:33-34) There is no higher authority.

Generally speaking, Sanctification has to do with my daily walk, and that will never be 100%. To try to merit or acheive this perfect standard can be maddening. To pursue this status of perfection, by human effort, will be tremendously frustrating and full of emotional anguish. Remember, justification is being saved! Sanctification is part of intentional discipleship. It is becoming Christ-like in our behavior and attitude. Big big difference!

This is where legalism is destructive. We should walk in harmony with our Heavenly Father. He wants us to be fruitful, and to live His life through us, but it will always be less than perfect. Accept that and you will be freer. You can save yourself a lot of frustration if you will keep these distinctions in mind. In justification we are absolutely and permanently accepted. In our walk, sanctification, we will have ups and down, and always less than perfect. We have a perfect Savior, but we as Christians will always be imperfect in our behavior.

Part of intentional discipleship is our sanctification. But is it far more than that! Our progress in sanctification manifests in practical terms, as we learn to walk by the Spirit. This is the process of learning to walk in harmony with the Holy Spirit, so we are spiritually mature in conduct. When we are walking accordingly, we are not fulfilling the desires of the flesh. (See Galatians, 5:22-26) However, there is more to discipleship than just our sanctification. There are a number of components. One is our righteous conduct. Our behavior. But there are many who are good moral believers, but lack a strong Biblical understanding. They have great zeal but lack grounding truth. They are limited to what they have been taught from the pulpit. And oftentimes that is lacking in doctrinal substance. They have not attained the Biblical knowledge necessary to defend the doctrines of the faith, so they are easily swayed by unbiblical teachings. To become Biblically literate requires diligent personal study to grasp the deeper doctrines of the faith. That only comes as the results of personal study of the scriptures and theologically sound resources. And that takes many years of discipline study. As the process continues, it should result in being both, spiritually mature and grounded in the doctrines of the faith. Manifesting Christ-like attributes, that is the desired goal for all Christians. Which only comes as part of being a growing and learning disciple. It also includes other aspects of the Christian life. Like the spiritual wisdom we gain, that can only come by the trials we experience in life. Those that test our faith in the real world. Life can be a great learning process, if we apply Biblical insights to the experiences of life. Which results in wisdom, our sanctification, and being able to be a discipling believer. All of which are necessary, if we want to be eternally impactful believers.

But this is conditioned on gaining the wisdom God wants us to learn, so we are prepared. Much of that can be learned by studying the wisdom books of the Bible, like Proverbs and Ecclesiastes. This is a desired goal for all believers; spiritual wisdom, the sanctification of our walk, and being grounded in the doctrines of the faith. Thereby, being a reflection of our Heavenly Father, which is all part of being a disciple. It is the growth of our faith process, and it takes time, but it is not automatic. It is a submission to the will of God, and walking accordingly. Always by the power and presence of the Holy Spirit, never in the power of our flesh, since the efforts of the flesh is equivalent to legalism. Which is deadly to our spiritual growth. The process and goal of sanctification is growing from a new babe in Christ, into a seasoned saint. This is the theme of the second half of the book of Galations, and addressed in many other parts of the scriptures.

Oftentimes, it includes learning to let go and leaving what is behind, behind. As Apostle Paul wrote in his book to the Philippians, in chapter 3. He learned to leave behind his sordid past and strive ahead toward the purpose of God in his life. He wrote that so we too can put that principle into practice. It is Godly wisdom to know that living in the past is not healthy, nor does it promote the spiritual life God desires for His children. Remember, the process of sanctification is a lifetime pursuit of learning and growing, and never ends. It always endeavors to have the mind of Christ. Moving from the past, our pre-Christian life, to the future that Christ has for us. Saint by position and growing saint like in our behavior.

This is why it is absolutely crucial to learn of my forever sonship. This is the foundation of stable freedom. This comes when I stop trying to earn God's love and just rest in it. When that takes place, we find freedom. For me, it manifested as I started to reckon on my eternal status as a child, and not my behavior to have this confidence. This is why the study and the acceptance of eternal security is so important. If something can change my status as a son, I have something to be terribly concerned about. A potential fear that I need to be anxious about. If I have to merit this salvation standing, then I will be insecure in my spiritual walk. It is the difference between living out my faith with assurance, and working to maintain the assurance of my salvation. A fear based salvation. Legalism! Yet, I understand the scriptures say equivalent to 365 times, not to fear. Seems to me like God wanted one reminder for everyday. And to fear not, would require a knowledge of my eternal security, for what greater fear could there ever be, but the fear of being separated from God for all of eternity.

This is where the body of Christ plays a major role in the sanctification and discipleship process. We need to be a body of believers, where real people can be open and honest with their real struggles. More than one person has reflected that attending church is not of interest, because they already are very mindful of their shortcomings, their personal failures.

When people are already overly conscious of their regrets and shame, they are not going to be interested in attending a church that is legalistic. Those who teach a conditional acceptance based on moral goodness, instead of Grace. We all need a Savior!

I was reflecting on this sometime back. If sermons become too focused on our shortcomings and the need for personal spiritual achievement, then there is no wonder why counseling centers are full. I visualized this as sitting in church with a bright life being focused on aspects of our lives that are deficient. Each week drawing attention to another area. The unrelenting call to measure up to an unachievable perfect standard. When this continues, it comes to the point that despair sets in. The feeling grows that we will never measure up to the proclaimed ideal standard. There will come a time when we just give up trying, resolving that that is an impossible goal, or are diminished to the point of feeling worthless. But if our acceptance is secure, because we understand we are permanent sons and daughters, beloved children of our Heavenly Father, we are then in a much better position to accept challenges to grow in grace. But the key is growing in GRACE. The result is our real sanctification. Then the natural desire is, we will want to be victors, because we are already victorious in Christ.

Let's think this through. The alternative is, if I think that my behavior is the basis of acceptance, there goes peace. This is a major difference. If I am reprimanded as a son but know I am secure because of the Father's love and promises, I can still have peace. Even when I am living contrary to some of the desires that our Heavenly Father has for us believers. However, If I am presented with the idea that my sonship is in question because of some deficiency in my Christian walk, then fear is the natural result. How could I not? Consequently, if my behavior is the condition for my eternity? I will experience recurring insecurity, to the point of affecting my mental health. Because any serious reflection, by any honest believer, will show that our lives do not always measure up to the goal of our faith, the sanctification of our lives. This is the affliction of legalism and probation salvation.

Here is the contrast. Before I was a Christian, I was sinning against a Holy God. He as the Judge of the universe must punish every sin. However, as a son, I am sinning against my Abba Father. But my sin issue has been atoned for and there is no need to punish. In another sense, this sin is more grievous, since it is my Daddy that I am sinning against. I am sinning against the One who loves me unconditionally. While, as a son, my status as a son is never in question, it is personally against Abba Father.

However, this does not mean that the church should accept willful defiance from regular attenders or members. The scriptures are clear that there is a code of expected conduct. Should there be a case when a fellow believer is walking in willful disobedience? There are Biblical principles to address this wayward believer. In general, the first is to confront the believer one on one, then if needed, as an elder group, and if that does not bring about the necessary change, the last step is putting one out of fellowship until they repent. Meaning he or she changes their minds on what is clearly unacceptable for a believer. During this period, we should pray for the believer. It is time for divine discipline. (1st Corinthians 5:5)

This is why accurate Biblical theology is so incredibly important. What is taught in our pulpits will either draw, or repulse people, who may be coming through the doors. We are not Christians because of our behavior. We are Christians because of our new identity in Christ. That should change our behavior, but not a condition for securing our salvation. (Again I refer to the doctrine statement in the Chafer Theology Seminary website, under, Soteriology)

We possess the ultimate truth. A sure foundation for living, and eternal truth. A church that does not hold up truth is close to being useless. We need to proclaim the truth. We have it as a divine revelation. But full of grace too. Yet this can be a difficult balance to achieve for the church. It is also a problem for many to find that balance in their own personal spiritual walk. How to hold strong morals, and still be a person or church that shows love as an extension of God's grace, can be difficult. For churches, a good sermon is not enough, we need relationships, and faith affirming theology.

This is why strongly grounded believers should be discipling other immature believers. (Functioning like a family) We as a church need mature believers, helping younger believers, in their role as husbands and wives. Mature saints, teaching men to be men, and a women on how to be a lady. We are so confused as a society. And this confusion is leaving men and women unsure of who they are, and their roles in life. Which leads to additional sexual confusion. And this is being injected into our society by those who reject the moral standards prescribed in the scriptures.

Therefore, the over-focusing on previous sinful behavior brings on unnecessary feelings of remorse. For those who previously bought into this permissive thinking, as they were led by these misguided philosophies of the world, need redeeming grace. Those whose lives have been marred by this persuasion, but now find themselves in need of restoring grace discipleship. On the alternative side of the issue, are those who continue in unrestrained, and unchecked, sexual freedom. A permissive mindset that has lost the value of wholesomeness. It is damaging to the person, primarily our young ladies. Creating confusion for both sexes. We need both, grace and truth. We can be holders of Biblical lifestyles, and still be merciful to the person who is struggling with the vices of life. Like Christ, who was a full manifestation of Grace and Truth.

This is best seen in the Gospel of John. Jesus is the true representative of truth and grace. It takes wisdom for the body of Christ to know how and when to apply. We want to be a body of believers that hold strong morals and also a place where sinners feel welcome. Overfocus on one will drive away the needy. Those already unduly sensitive to their past sinful failures. To be lenient on the teaching of the other brings loose morals and a lifestyle that is not acceptable for a child of God. Both legalism and loose morals can be destructive. It is like being a spiritual coach. We need encouragement, and to be challenged, to grow in grace, with the emphasis on Grace. A teaching that can see that all throughout the New Testament. The writers of the NT epistles generally established the secure foundation of a believer, before the therefore, challenges to grow in the faith. (See Ephesians the early chapters)

(I am thankful I have good solid Christian friends that I can share my spiritual struggles with. They keep me balanced. They encourage me like Barnabas for Paul).

Grace and truth together. A needed but sometimes difficult balance to achieve. An additional reason to know your security in Christ. But also our need to understand the Heavenly Father's discipline and the Bema Seat judgment. (Both will be discussed in upcoming chapters) All the while, never neglecting the need to keep the freeness of the gospel clear. This without losing the understanding that God is immutable holy, even as our

Heavenly Father. We are now in a different relationship that is sure, a son with his Father, eternally secure. The truth is that we are eternally secure, but have a Heavenly Father who is desiring us to grow in sanctification. So when I need correction, I am receiving it from my Abba Father, and not the unloving rebuke from a God who conditions my being in a salvation relationship, that is based on my faithfulness. (Merit based salvation) This conditional God is not our Father. (Grace relationship)

The desire of God for all of His children is that we grow mature as sons and daughters, but not on our own. We are to live according to the leading of the Spirit and never on our own fleshly power. Which is often a sign of legalism. Trying to live up to some standard to earn God's acceptance will never work. We need to learn the teachings of Galatians 5, so we don't walk according to the flesh, but manifest the qualities of the Spirit by walking in the Spirit.

(My editorial) The age we live in is very difficult. We have many in society pushing for absolute moral freedom. Usually in the realm of unchecked sexual expressions. The idea that a man can use a shower room that my daughter or wife is in need of, angers me. Just because a man is confused about his sexuallity does not give him the right to violate my wife, or daughters, modesty and moral purity. Their safety is in question and their modesty is compromised. But is it being pushed upon us! To object to what is being pushed upon us often brings accusations of being intolerant. It will be a wonder if we will be able to find anything wrong with any moral choice in the emerging society. What happened to the long held virtue of wholesomeness. A lost virtue. Where is the wholesome lady in a dress? The gentleman who is faithful and kind. I am sure those pushing these ideas have private bathrooms. I'm sure the Speaker of the House is not sharing her personal facilities with her male representatives. I am sure if I visited the capital of our county, I could not use her shower while she was in her private domain. The hypocrisy is astonishing. The propagation of immorality and calling it equality or tolerance is unconscionable. God forbid. All morality is either based on personal preferences or divine revelation. If we keep compromising on moral issues, we will eventually have nothing left to hold as truly wholesome, nothing sacred. This is social engineering without a moral reference point. No place to plant our feet on what is right or wrong. Keep on reading to develop these thoughts.

CHAPTER 19

Eternal Security and the spiritual stability of the believer

As discussed in the last chapter, it is essential to understand our standing and security in Christ, if I am to experience steady peace and joy in my Christian walk! I have recommended a number of very good books that I found instrumental in my spiritual journey. But seven in particular need to be highlighted in regards to this chapter. (Shall Never Perish, Forever by Dennis M. Rokser, Once Saved Always Saved by R.T. Kendall, Shall Never Perish by J. F. Strombeck, Secure Forever by Thomas M.Cucuzza, Eternal Security by Charles Stanley, Getting the Gospel Wrong by J. B. Hixson, and How You Can Be Sure That You Will Spend Eternity with God by Erwin W. Lutzer) So I am not going to spend a lot of time arguing for the acceptance of Eternal Security. They do it so much better than I could. My intent is to give a few arguments, and then leave those interested in learning more about the subject, to the reading of those suggested books. Additionally, these arguments are woven throughout this book. These are just some highlights to refresh your memory. While not an exhaustive section of the book, this is extremely important for the spiritual well being of the believer. Unfortunately, avoided by most because it is believed to be unnecessarily controversial. But all truth is controversial, so regardless of opinion, I believe it is absolutely crucial to have this understanding, in order for Christians to have full confidence in their eternal destiny. It is also absolutely crucial in order to have a settled peaceful assurance! I can be assured because it is the promise of God that I am depending on and not my feeble efforts. Let's continue with some of the affirming principles....

Frequently in the Bible, the offer of salvation is conditioned on believing on Jesus Christ and His sacrificial atonement on the cross, which results in receiving the gift of eternal life. Seems pretty simple to me. Somehow we complicate simple issues. When this is not the accepted teaching we drift into uncertainty about our salvation. Which brings about spiritual depression, as noted by J. F. Strombeck, in his book on Eternal Security. The spiritual depression results from the uncertainty regarding the nature of gift. If a human contribution is required? Then confidence will always be lacking. Because any human contribution will always be subject to uncertainty. But this is not the description of salvation the Bible describes. The Bible describes the condition for eternal salvation, and its permanent results, differently from the hopes for personal sanctification. (The justification and sanctification descriptions in chapter 18)

The confirmation for this may be best seen in the Gospel of John, chapter 5 verse 24. Look at the progression of thought. It starts with Jesus making a promise to the one who hears and believes, with the results being eternal life. Which is in the present tense. Meaning I am currently in possession of the gift. The promise continues with an assurance of never coming into condemnation, and already crossing over from death to life. A passage that indicates the conditions for receiving salvation, and continues with explaining some of the salvation results. These results fall under the umbrella of the numerous salvation benefits we received at the moment of faith. Seems pretty clear, and personally, very comforting to me. Maybe why it is one of my favorite passages in the Bible. Certainly much different from probation salvation teachings, which most often are derived as a result of not interpreting passages in proper context. Often those that confuse sanctification passages, where a commitment or behavior change is implied, in contrast with justification salvation passages, that are final and complete.

As noted, for years I was a probation officer. There were conditions of probation. Once those conditions were met the probationer was released and set free from those conditions. They generally earned their "salvation" from probation by good behavior. This is not so with the free offer of

God. The offer of salvation is an offer to receive the free gift of eternal life. Remember that the teachings from God's authors have intended meaning. Therefore, the scriptural revelations from God, is that receiving eternal life, is receiving life that is eternal in duration. That alone should end the discussion. One is not on probation with God! An unbeliever upon understanding the gospel, and believing it, has been given eternal life. It is a present possession for the one who has come to faith. A new standing of forever sonship/daughtership. It is received at the very moment of faith and results in being granted the free gift of salvation. We don't wait to verify it with proof of good works. It is not to be earned in part as we walk out the faith. (The sanctifying aspect of the Christian experience) We are justified the moment we accept what Christ did on our behalf. This is a full permanent acceptance, and not probationary or conditional acceptance.

As noted, not to believe this will result in an uncertain salvation and/ or spiritual depression. Furthermore, it also affects our boldness. If my salvation is conditional, I tend to live defensively, trying to play it safe and maintain or protect my salvation status. I may forgo steps of bold faith, because I am afraid that I may encounter a situation that puts the status of my salvation at risk. For example, let's say that I am put into a situation where I must choose between potential persecution and/or hardship, or the safety of a loved one, and by compromising my faith because of fear, or because of my love for a family member, I have in essence denied Christ, and therefore I lose my salvation. (That is an implied potential consequence of probation salvation thinking) I may therefore, instinctively, shy away from those situations. I naturally stay in my comfort zone to avoid any chance of this dilemma. Living in protective fear. In that line of thinking, my salvation status is maintained because of my faithful endurance, and not the assured promise from God. However, if I know I am absolutely saved, and what is afforded to me is an absolute promise from God, then what do I have to fear? At most, temporal discomfort, which if I endure, will bring about eternal blessings. (More on that in chapter 21)

Moreover, there are numerous teachings in the scripture that reinforce this principle of our secure salvation. Consider what the scriptures teach about being born again, or becoming a new creation of God. How can one be born again and then become unborn? Or, become a new creation then

121

reverting back to their former status. This teaching is foreign to the clear teaching of scriptures. The scriptures continue to reinforce that security theme with the teaching that we have been sealed by the Holy Spirit until the day of our redemption. There is no one in the universe that is able to undo what God the Holy Spirit has done in sealing the new believer for the day of his heavenly arrival. Once saved, always saved. Or, once sealed, always sealed. A promise that is absolutely dependable because it is based on God's immutable perfect character. God cannot lie, it is contrary to His nature.

There is another scriptural teaching that is often not translated in most scriptures. It has been drawn out by Dennis Rokser in his book, Shall Never Perish, Forever. It is called a double negative. There are a number of places in the Bible (Gospel of John) where translators do not record the double negative (ou me), which in the Greek means it will never happen under any circumstance. It is not proper English to translate as such. So it is not translated in most modern translations, but very reassuring to know as a believer. It is emphasized in Greek, with the idea, that we will never lose our salvation under any circumstance. It may appear redundant and not the customary usage in English, but in the Greek, it is an emphatic assurance. It is certainly a Biblical teaching we need to know, since it adds to the assurance of our faith walk. What a wonderful assurance, to have this comprehension of our absolute security of our salvation, that no matter what happens in life, I know that I know my eternal destiny. May I say that the book by Rokser is excellent. I have read it at least five times. Dr. Andy Woods also does an excellent series that can be found on the church's website. (SLBC Andy Woods, under the topic Soteriology) A 58 week teaching on salvation. I strongly recommend the investment of time listening to this series by Dr. Woods and the reading of the book by Pastor Rokser.

I liked to explain it this way while teaching in the jail. (since they were prisoners this made particular sense) Every unsaved person will someday stand before an infinity Holy God. He as Judge knows everything about everything in one's life, even the intent of the heart and motives. Even those that are generally noble, will be put to test. We can hide nothing from God's all knowing mind. This knowledge is the evidence against us, and then that evidence is applied to the standard, which is absolute perfection of God Himself. There are no alterations to that perfection. As noted numerous times, in this book, the holy standard is the immutable and intrinsic nature of who God is as God. And be judged. And judge fairly. And found unworthy. Unless, they have been declared righteous by the ultimate Judge, and therefore, they have become benefactors of the declaration of our justification, Christ's righteousness applied. (Romans 5:1 and 8:33-34)

Therefore, those who accept the gift of eternal salvation have changed their forever position. The one believing, is now a forever son or daughter, of their Heavenly Father. We will never ever face God as the Judge. We have changed rooms. We are no longer in the courtroom of life waiting for the pending judgment of God, where perfect justice must be administered. We have been granted, or better said, placed into the forever family room of our Heavenly Father. The heaven or hell judgment is over. We no longer need to fear that someday we will face, once again, the question of our eternal destiny. There has been an irrevocable change into that of being a son or daughter of our Abba Father. We have been accepted into the forever family room of our Heavenly Father. We have the complete freedom from the ultimate fear.

However, we do not escape our responsibilities with our Heavenly Father. As Christians, our Heavenly Father wants us to be living ambassadors. To behave like sons/daughters of the coming Savior. I like to explain it this way; let's suppose I have two sons. (I don't so this is an acceptable illustration. So on with my illustration) One of my sons is always going astray. He just cannot seem to avoid trouble. He is often an embarrassment to the family. As expected, our family name is important to us. We desire a good reputation in the church, our neighborhood, and with the larger community. Now, my other son brings great joy to us. He is a fine young man. He makes us proud that he has our name. We frequently hear from those in the community what a responsible young man he is. He works hard and is honest in his endeavors.

Now comes Friday night. The two sons of mine come asking for money for their Friday night activities. The first son who tends to be reckless with those expectations of ours as a son, and who simply cannot be trusted, because it seems that everytime I grant his request, he disappoints us, therefore, I deny him. (In the Christian experience this could be a loss of blessing, Fatherly discipline, or unanswered prayers to name a few) I simply do not want to contribute to another embarrassing and drunken night of shame. Not when he disrespects our name by his behavior. However, the well behaved son, the trustworthy one, I gladly give him money as a reward for another good week in school, and as an appreciation of his behavior, therefore, the request was granted. (In the Christian experience that may be represented as an answer to prayer or some particular blessing from our Heavenly Father or those rewards at the Bema Seat) In this illustration, it may be money for pizza and activities with his friends. He has earned this, and I want to show him my appreciation for his representing the Miller name with dignity. Oftentimes blessings come to those who are faithful in their walk. Just because God loves to bless His children.

So sonship is never the question. (The illustration represents our degree of fellowship with our Heavenly Father) It is the quality of my relationship with my sons, or lack thereof, but there is never a question of sonship. They were both born to me and forever my sons. It is only the quality of the relationship with my sons that is in question. This too is the Christian life. Once a son always a son. Since eternal life is forever life, sonship is forever. Once born into a family, always a member of the family. (For the record we have one son of whom I am very proud to be his dad. A really fine young man)

This teaching is highlighted by two of the writings of Apostle John. In the Gospel of John, the primary focus is on establishing the nature of Christ deity, and His saving work, conditioned on faith and faith alone. Where faith in Jesus Christ and the acceptance of His payment on the cross for our sins, results in eternal life. Whereas, in the 1st letter of John, he writes more about having fellowship with our Heavenly Father. How to walk in a manner that brings one into a harmonious fellowship. They do have some crossover, but the main focus is different in the two books. While the truth of our secure position is established at the moment of salvation, it does not release us from consequences. As I have experienced in my own life. God has a strong disciplining hand for His wayward children. (See chapter 12 of Hebrews) While His discipline can be harsh, even to the point of premature termination of our physical life form of discipline, it never nullifies our eternal life and new birth. The discomfort that is experienced by the hand of our Heavenly Father means He loves us. He also wants us to be fruitful and exhibit qualities of His Son, our Savior. Even in discipline, God is expressing His love. Actually, this is a demonstration of love, He disciplines those He loves. This can be done without loss of salvation, since He is fully satisfied with the payment made almost 2,000 years ago on the cross. Furthermore, in addition to those who received the benefits of sonship, always remember that we are clothed in the very righteousness of Christ, he will not disrobe us.

A few last thoughts on this subject. This relates to God's immutable holiness. Let's say one was saved but not eternally secure, what happens the very moment a believer sins? Let's say someone is saved at church one Sunday but the moment he gets ready to leave he has a sinful thought. Then the newly saved person is distracted by someone. The sinning thought is later forgotten. Has the sin nullified his salvation? Does this sin nullify his new birth requiring him to be saved again? What degree of sin would it take? Remember, the immutable nature of God does not ever change. I have never met one person who is not a sinner, even after salvation. Therefore, any sin no matter how minute, would cause God's standards to be reviolated, thereby, potentially outside the previous salvific work of Christ, if the benefits of our coming to saving faith do not have permanent results. What a horrible situation to consider. If our salvation is a probationary status or conditional? Any sin would be enough to nullify our salvation and we would be in need of being saved again and again and again, you get the point.

The logical outcome of this probation salvation thinking is that before salvation, every sin had to be atoned for, but after salvation, God lowers His standards and accepts some sin. But this idea has no place in the scriptures. There is no place that God says you can go so far, then once you transgress this limit, you lose the benefits of what Christ accomplished on the cross. To think this way would create an uncertainty that could cause madness, or degrees of spiritual depression. If one truly considers the implications, it is troubling to the soul! The belief in eternal security is necessary for our spiritual and mental stability. And is theologically consistent with what the Bible teaches.

The expectation that there should be some moral reform after salvation is true. Nonetheless, the issue is the absolute completeness of salvation. If after being saved, I enter probation salvation status, then this dilutes the holiness of God. Meaning, he modifies His requirements of absolute required holiness for salvation to continue. It would then be a combination of His works and/or my moral behavior, in my post salvation, to sustain the continuance of my salvation. No assurance there. Also there is no litmus test in the scriptures for this thinking. There are indicators of our spiritual development but never for our eternal salvation. The key to proper interpretation is the audience. To whom are those particular scriptural passages addressing? For unbelievers, the standard is absolute perfect holiness, that is why a completed salvation is needed. We need a declaration of permanent justification. For the believer, calls for a more righteous walk with our Father, a more sanctified lifestyle as a son/daughter. And that requires commitment to walking in the Spirit. Because justification has taken place and never needs to be repeated, since sonship is the new eternal status. Therefore, behavior is a fellowship question, and not a salvation issue.

A few more thoughts. If probation salvation is the status of the Christian, then someone may need to be reborn again and again and again to keep rejoining the family of God. Some claim the teaching of 1 John is the required solution to restore salvation after sinning. One would need to confess sin to be restored back to salvation status. However, no one is totally mindful of every sin. We may need to confess known sin to restore our fellowship with the Father, as we are convicted by the Holy Spirit or from reading the Bible, but never to restore sonship. We need to walk in the light of God's revelation and confess known sins, because we want to have His blessings, and be in close loving fellowship. Furthermore, to be in good fellowship with our Heavenly Father, helps us find favor in our prayer life, etc. But obedience is never required to sustain our sonship, since new birth is permanent.

This in particular is why we need to understand our forever settled salvation to have emotional stability. One that is not subject to nullification. A secure salvation that has the very promise of God behind the guarantee. This is the emotional freedom of knowing our secure hope in Christ. The sure hope that I am in a forever relationship with my Abba Father. The predicament of facing the Judgeship of God is over, forever.

To fail to understand this likely means we have not thought through the implications of this teaching, as would be the case with probation salvation theology. And the fear that this belief naturally suggests. Because, if we are not thinking through the lodgical ramifications of the probation status teaching, with the mindset that understands the absolute immutable holiness of God, and we don't believe in eternal security, we will never have complete assurance of heaven. We would at best have a hopeful salvation. We will never have the absolute assured confidence of our sonship with our Abba Father. A sure confidence that we can always approach the throne of our Father because of God's grace, because we are His children. We need an understanding of our irrevocable gift of eternal salvation to be spiritually and emotionally anchored.

That is why the scriptures describe our salvation in many diverse terms. Like being born again, declared justified, clothed in the very righteousness of God, being sealed by the Holy Spirit, and possessing eternal life. All of which indicate our acceptance and standing has forever changed. Our sonship is one that ensures our eternal future. This is the forever change of status, from a son of Adam, to a child of our Abba Father. Therefore, to doubt our salvation is detrimental to our growth. If I can lose eternal life? What was it that I received? Our heavenly Father wants us to know the assurance that we are forever His! (1 John chapter 5) It is the foundation of emotional security. This is why it is written in the fellowship book of 1st John. If we are uncertain of our eternal status with our Heavenly Father, then true fellowship will evade us.

I could anticipate some of the objections to this teaching. Those who claim that one must be an active disciple to be a Christian. But that would mean that my faithfulness is a condition for salvation. That I must do good works to validate or contribute to my salvation. But this thinking minimizes Christ's completed work on the cross. Which Jesus says was finished. (John 19:30) Furthermore, discipleship is not always a good indicator. Judas was a disciple (a learner of Christ), but not born again. (John 17:12) Even though he was a disciple for years, he was the son of perdition. (Read chapter 13 of the Gospel of John and well discussed by Rokser, in chapter 12, of his book on Eternal Security) And in the Gospel of Matthew, it was said it would have been better if he was never born. (Matthew chapter 26) Lastly, let me ask you a very serious question; Can you really say you are a disciple, if you are not active in the great commission as commanded? (Matthew 28:19-20) Will you apply this principle for yourself, if you are not sharing your faith, and allow people to go to Hell, and then claim that discipleship is a requirement for salvation? We should look for opportunities to share our faith, it is commanded. But discipleship is not a condition for our salvation, because it adds human obedience to the salvific work of Christ. The scriptures are clear, it is not by works, so it may be by grace. (Titus 3:5) Our discipleship should be expected, but not a condition for salvation. If it were, then should not those sins of omission, like evangelism, be included in the requirements?

Our motivation should result from an understanding of the implication of the faith, knowing the consequences of accepting or rejecting the faith. It is a true expression of our love for our fellow man. And our love for mankind is what moves us to evangelism. Furthermore, our motivations to share our faith, shows how much we really truly believe what we profess.

Lastly, as I have noted, to doubt our status is to live in spiritual uncertainty. I need to know that I know that I am a child forever of the living God. He is now my eternal Father. Never to be put aside as a son or daughter. That is comforting joy my friend. A real peaceful joy! NO matter what happens in this evil world, my rightful standing as a child in the family room of God is never in question. Because, I am adopted, redeemed, born again, a new creation, justified, a present possessor of eternal life, and therefore, I will be glorified. Guaranteed! What do I really need to fear? Hallelujah, what a Savior, for whom I am thankful for my all-encompassing salvation.

Mini Bibliography for this chapter

1. Strombeck, J. F. *Shall Never Perish,* Kregel Publications, 1991
2. Rokser, Dennis M. *SHALL NEVER PERISH, Forever.* Grace Gospel Press, 2012
3. Cucuzza, Thomas M. *Secure forever!* WWW.xulonpress.com, 2007
4. Kendall, R.T. *Once Saved, Always Saved.* Authentic Media, 2005
5. Stanley, Charles. *Eternal Security*, Thomas Nelson Publishers 1990

6. Lutzer Erwin W. *How You Can Be Sure That You Will Spend Eternity with God,* Moody Press,1996

7. Hixson, J. B. Ge*tting the Gospel Wrong,* Grace Gospel Press, 2013

8. Olson, Lloyd A. *Eternal Security, Once Saved Always Saved,* Tate Publishing and Enterprises, 2007

9. Dr. Andy Woods Soteriology series found at SLBC Andy Woods

10. And numerous other books. See some of them in my Bibliography section

11. Lightner, Robert P. *Sin, the Savior and Salvation,* Thomas Nelson, 1991

12. Stegall, Thomas L. *The Gospel of the Christ,* 2009

CHAPTER 20

Eternal Security and the Gospel presentation

When endeavoring to share the gospel with the lost, it is crucial not only to present a clear message of the gospel content, but also, to be able to communicate the salvific benefits that come as the results of believing. It is a process of learning that takes time and careful study. But it is absolutely necessary for those receiving the salvation message, to know the results of believing, so they have a firm confidence in their salvation. Therefore, to share a faulty gospel has eternal repercussions. First, because a faulty gospel is ineffective to save gospel. Secondly, a faulty understanding of the results of believing the gospel, results in an uncertain salvation. This is addressed in the first chapter of Galatians by the Apostle Paul. Where there is curse, an anathema, for altering the gospel message or its content. Why so harsh? Because it is a message that has eternal consequences. In the Galatian letter, Paul warned them that there were individuals who were influencing others by altering the Gospel. They were teaching that there were other conditions that must be met to earn their right standing, both in justification and growing sanctification. The altered message had become a confusing message. They were actually very diligent in the pursuit of righteousness. But it was an attempt at man-made righteousness. Which falls woefully short of the infinite righteness needed for acceptance before God, and does not result in eternal sonship. This is a grievous substitution for the righteousness provided by God, through the person and work of Christ. Later, as the book of Galatians progresses, Paul starts to address how to grow in sanctification salvation. The process of growing mature in their given salvation. How to grow from a new babe in Christ into a fruitful mature believer, which requires a living faith.

Whereas, in comparison with the book for 1st Corinthians, when Paul is addressing immoral behavior, he gives a list of warnings and potential consequences, but no anthama. Why? Because it is not how people establish a right status with God. Serious lifestyle issues for sure, but not the altering of the message that brings eternal life. The apostle Paul, who wrote both books, had greater concern for those self-righteous alterations to the gospel in Galatians, than he does for carnal behavior in 1st Corinthians. The church of today has this backwards. While sinning behavior has significant consequences. Paul was far more concerned about the eternal consequences of a faulty gospel message. Since there is only one message that brings eternal salvation. The development of Christlikeness in the life of a believer is significant but pales in comparison with the requirements for the gift of eternal life. There will be a lot of self-righteous people having the doors of heaven closed to them. The standard does not change. It is absolute perfection that is required, and nothing less is acceptable. This is why we need a permanent solution for our unrighteous condition. Being clothed in the very righteousness of Christ is just one aspect of the solution.

I am not saying that failing to teach the assurance of eternal security, it is not possible to present the gospel. However, there is the very real possibility that some expected works contribution may be implied in the message, and confuse the message. This is an alteration of the true gospel. This altered Gospel does not lead to eternal life. The whole reason for sharing the gospel is to lead someone into a saving faith. (This is not a special faith but a properly placed faith) That requires clarity, and proper content.

If there are any requirements added to the freeness of gospel, it is faulty, and may lead to devastating eternal consequences. We must be diligent that what we are sharing is God's truth, nothing but the truth, and the message is clear and understandable. This is not a trivial theological issue. We are talking about God's only plan of redemption. There is one gospel. There is one Lord and Savior who was qualified to bring about the salvation of mankind. It was His work as Lord, on the cross, that atoned for our sins. If you are failing to understand these principles you are not grasping the distance between you and the infinitely holy God. You do not understand the gospel! Don't fool yourself. Pride is very destructive and can have eternal consequences. If you think you can somewhat help merit standing before God, you will be eternally disappointed. That is being kind-hearted in description. The litmus test I gave remains true.

There is another significant issue in a gospel message that does not include full assurance. That is, until the message has been delivered, understood and accepted, it is subject to misunderstanding. The understanding that is necessary, is that we, upon believing, have a secure and everlasting life. Until that takes place we will naturally experience frequent bouts of doubt. This is not the same as the proper respect for God fear. But recurring thoughts of not being saved, or returning to the state of the unsaved, because of some deficient moral behavior. It is also possible that one may have never actually been saved, because there remains questions as to what is really required to be saved. A nagging fear that you are not measuring up to the requirements of salvation. Of course, if you are trying to merit salvation, either in part or as a whole by your own merits, then it is a well placed fear. You then have valid reasons to question your salvation. This is the dangerous, but deceitful message of you cooperating with God to earn salvation, like those, to whom Paul is writing to warn in Galatians. Which is so prevalent in many church doctrines today, and often preached erroneously from pulpits! Regardless of what aspects of your responsibility you undertake in the effort to help secure salvation, your part will be subject to defect. Woefully deficient. And the agony of missing the true gospel will last for eternity.

Remember, the standing sonship/daughtership requirement before God is always 100% or not at all. When it comes to our salvation, there is only pure white or absolute blackness, there is no gray. This failure to understand the finality of our salvation naturally leads to uncertainty. And not the peace that our Father wants us to enjoy. And rightly so! The understanding of our eternal sonship/daughtership is the only way to have true peace. If you doubt your eternal standing, how can you possibly present a gospel that gives assurance to the unbeliever. How will they even know if they are saved?

As indicated, we can share the salvation message without teaching eternal security, but it will always be an unreliable message. And one that is subject to insecurity for the one believing the message. My recommendation is that we include the assurance of salvation when presenting the gospel of Jesus Christ. It is always a cleaner and more confident message to share. And will likely produce a more lasting assurance for the one believing. And, a more joyful response. A joyful response, knowing that, upon receiving the unconditional (other than faith alone) and complete salvation, granted to them in Christ, they can rest assured. It comes down to this simple equation; either Christ paid it all, or we have an uncertain and untrustworthy salvation. These equations have real ramifications. One option can affect our spiritual health. The other, spurs us on to a Savior, to whom we are so grateful, that we want to worship. This is not a trivial question to answer.

For what resting hope is there to a gospel presentation that is uncertain in its secureness? To present the idea that by believing you are saved, but don't count on it. A gospel that suggests that you need to prove it by your behavior is insecurity at best, and maddening at worst. Of course, if you want others to take your conversion seriously, a change of behavior brings credibility to the inward change in your life. But we also see that outward change for many in cults. Outward moral reform is not a dependable test of salvation. We need to keep the gospel clear, faith alone, in the work of Christ alone, brings forgiveness of sin and eternal life. We as a body of believers are not presenting a confident message, nor does it appear at times, we even trust our own message.

Have you seen the books being marketed that claim to bring assurance of salvation. Why is it that after reading them, the end result is that the reader is left so uncertain? It is because those authors add and add subjective requirements, and then suggest these subjective litmus tests of our behavior brings assurance. Puzzling, is it not! All of those are subjective requirements that don't bring assurance. Keep it clear, upon simple trusting faith in the person, and sacrifice of Jesus Christ, brings forgiveness of sin, acceptance into the forever family of God, and eternal life. Additional details may be needed to help clarify the subject, but never more subjective qualifications.

In summary, if we do not have the confident peace that we are safe and secure, how do we share a sure and confident salvation message? If we ultimately do not know if we are eternally saved without a doubt? How is the one receiving our message to know? Let's be clear with the gospel! Both with the content and results. Because when we have this uncertainty of where we stand with our Heavenly Father, our motivations for living out our faith are different. It is based on working to maintain our salvation and not a resting confidence in our salvation. Protective salvation versus bold living salvation. Almost like the experience of foster homes for so many children. They are living there, but they know that it is not likely to be their permanent home. We don't have a foster home God. We need to communicate that the acceptance of Christ, results in the permanent removal from the courtroom into the living room. A permanent acceptance into the forever family of our Abba Father. Eternal security is the assurance that I am forever, and ever, His child. This is the essence of what the gospel means. A gift in the truest sense. One that is eternal in duration. That is why the gospel is offensive. It is a claim of exclusively. There are alot of gray areas in our lives, this should not be one of them. There is only one way, John 14:6, and it is an exclusive way!

Mini Bibliography

1. Bing, Charles C. *Lordship Salvation,* Ph.D. Dissertation, 1991
2. Bing, Charles C. *Simply By Grace,* Kregel Publishing, 2009
3. Bing, Charles C. *Grace Salvations and Discipleship,* Grace Theology Press, 2015
4. Chafer, Lewis Sperry, *Salvation,* Kregel Publications, 1991
5. Chafer, Lewis Sperry, *True Evangelism,* Kregel Publications, 1993
6. Chafer, Lewis Sperry, *Grace,* Kregel Publications, 1995
7. Cocoris, G. Michael, *The Salvation Controversy,* Insights From the Word, 2008
8. Hixson, J. B. *The Gospel Unplugged, Lucidbook,* 2011
9. Hixson, J. B., Whitmire, Rick, Zuck, Roy B. *Freely By His Grace,* Grace Gospel Press, 2012
10. Hixson, J. B. G*etting the Gospel Wrong,* Grace Gospel Press, 2013
11. Hixson, J. B. *Top 10 Reasons some people go to Hell, and One Reason No One Ever Has To!* Grace Acres Press, 2020
12. Moyer, R. Larry, *Free and Clear,* Kregel Publications, 1997

CHAPTER 21

The eternal consequences for the believer at the Bema Seat of Christ

If what I have written so far is true? And I am convinced it is! (Or I would not be writing this book) I understand, and expect, that many will disagree with me on certain aspects of my theology. But I stand by what has been composed. But I can surmise the objections, there are no consequences for bad living, this is not true. There are significant consequences. Even eternal ones, but our eternal salvation is not one of them. At the Bema Seat of Christ, the quality of our Christian lives will be evaluated. Whether we were faithful in our role as an ambassador of Christ, or neglectful in our given responsibilities, it will be revealed.

For some reason, this teaching about the Bema Seat has been neglected by the majority of pastors. And the ramifications of this subject have failed to be expounded upon from the pulpit. Yet, it is a central teaching in regards to the consequences that result from how we live out this gift of our salvation. It pertains to the quality of our Christian walk, and gives us even more motivation to live faithfully, as a child of God. The Apostle Paul writes about the subject a number of times. (See 1st Corinthians 3:12-15, 2 Corinithians 5:10 and Romans 15:10, as examples of a few) In just about every book in the New Testament some form of warning and/or promised reward, is given to the Chrisitian regarding the consequences of how they are living out the faith. It may also come to the faithful one, with a warning not to lose what you have labor for, etc. The idea being that you have lived a quality Christian life, don't allow a temptation or moral compromise, to cause you to lose much of your testimony and/or reward at the Bema Seat. (1st Corinthians 9:24-27 as an example of the Apostle Paul's desire not to become disqualified or lose a well earned reward) There are both positive and negative aspects of this concept. These are not warnings of loss of salvation, but losing grace rewards because of unfaithful living.

The idea that every believer will be given the same position in heaven is without Biblical collaboration. To believe that the truly born again, but comfortable Christian, will receive the same reward as the missionary who sacrificially pursued the cause of Christ is just not Biblical. The Lord is a just God, and will not forget anyone's sacrificial labor. While salvation is absolutely free, our God is just, and will reward accordingly those who took seriously the responsibilities of being an ambassador of Christ. For those who lived their lives in light of eternity, and not for temporary pleasures, will find a great reward at the Bema Seat. Those who avoided sharing the gospel to avoid social stigma will find they have forsaken eternal reward opportunities. Those eternal blessings that could have been theirs, if they were willing to take seriously, the central message of the Bible.

If a pastor wants to motivate his sheep, he should highlight the results of the gospel, and the rewards for being faithful in that ambassador mission. Pastors willingly accepted this calling to teach and preach. Therefore it should mean the whole counsel of scriptures. As the Apostle Paul is recorded as saying in the 20th chapter of Acts.

Sadly, many of the pulpits of our day are adrift with appeasement of conscience, diligent not to offend. The major theme in the Sunday morning message has emerged into the popular message of how to live successfully in this transitory life. Often embedded in this message is an emphasis on overcoming trials that naturally come to all of us. Within this teaching, is the idea that success in this life is the goal. Those under this teaching may feel better, and find worldly success, but that does not have much impact on eternity.

The results of this prevailing message being preached is that one can have their best life now. This diminishes the motivation to live with the thought that one's personal sacrifices will be remembered, and rewarded, in the coming Kingdom. What happened to the willing sacrifice for the cause of Christ? Knowing that one's labors will be recognized by God at the Bema Seat. The confidence that God will see their good deeds, as an expression of their faith, and reward them in the ages to come. Remember, that God placed this teaching before the believer, so we can know our sacrificial labors will be rewarded. This was His revelation to us! Furthermore, it reveals His fairness to each and every believer, that our God is a just Heavenly Father. Unfortunately, many Christians will be greatly disappointed when they realize that by pursuing temporal amusements, which have ended at death, has resulted in forfeiting possible heavenly rewards, because they were not diligent in the greater aspects of the faith.

How did we fall into a misguided emphasis in the church? Where key Biblical truths are neglected. We simply are not being taught key Biblical truths in many churches. This neglect of Biblical truth undermines our motivation for service. It also manifests in the benign impact of many believers in our local church bodies. Since, if there is no reward, or eternity is not dependent on the truthfulness of John 14:6, then soft Christianity makes sense. It is comfortable to the soul but deadly to the mission to proclaim the gospel.

So let's explore this teaching to establish its relevance for the Christian. Remember, this is a Christian only evaluation, there is no question of heaven or hell at the Bema Seat. It takes place in heaven after the Rapture of the body of Christ. The evaluation has to do with service and sacrifice. What did I do with the knowledge of the faith? What was I willing to sacrifice for the cause of Christ? Was I willing to sacrifice some of my desired social reputation to reach those outside the faith? Was I diligent in my effort to reach those that need instructions, and then encouragement, on how to join the forever family? When it comes to rewards, some of the questions are; did I sacrifice anything for the faith? Did I manifest Christ-like attributes in my personal life? Was I a faithful servant? Did I understand the perilous situation the lost are facing? And then have diligent motivation to introduce them to the hope we have in Christ? Am I being accurate with the gospel presentation?

Dr. J. B. Hixson and Mark Fontecchio, in their book WHAT LIES AHEAD, A Biblical overview of the end times, listed a number of the areas that Christ will evaluate at the judgment seat. It is a very comprehensive list. These areas are; Enduring Trials, Diligently Seeking God, Perseverance, Faithful in Ministry, Longing for Christ's Appearance, Leading Other to Christ, Faithfulness to Christ, Diligence in the Christain Walk, Stewardship of what Has Been Entrusted to Us, Enduring Persecution, Remaining in Close Fellowship with Christ, Benevolence toward the Poor, Wholehearted Service to Christ and Ministering to the Saints. They give a thorough and detailed overview of this aspect of the Christian Bema Seat evaluation. Others give a different detailed list. But in general they are the same similar areas of evaluation. Depending on who is listing them, and how they are classified, will determine the categories. But the key point is that our God is not unjust to forget our struggles or sacrifices, in our service for the cause of Christ. Our degree of motivation also shows the degree of hope we have in Christ. We usually only go as far as we have the confidence that what we believe is really and truly, true. Hence the need to study apologetics and solid doctrine, which affirms that we are investing in what is really worthwhile. Our devotion in the joyful service to others manifest the Love of Christ that dwells in our hearts. A sacrificial life shows that we are truly eternally minded. Our sacrifice for the cause of Christ further shows we really believe our faith is true. It exhibits that we understand that how we live does matter both now and into eternity.

As you would expect, the evaluation will be different for each individual in the body of Christ, depending on the opportunities and situations. It further depends on the calling that God gave and the obedience to the call. Not everyone has the same talents and responsibilities placed on them. Not everyone is called to be a pastor or evangelist. For those who are called to these roles, the requirements are higher, but the reward is also greater for those called to these high callings, assuming they are faithful in that calling.

As an example regarding Pastors, there is a particular reward for faithful Pastors and teachers. But as expected, they are also held to higher standards. (See the Pastor letters of Paul, 1st and 2nd Timothy and Titus) Higher expectations from the Lord are due to the elevated role in the body of Christ, and therefore, the reason for this should be clear. Should John Q Christian have a moral failure, the impact is generally limited to his personal testimony and family. It does impact the message of the gospel, but not to the degree of a pastor. A smaller impact has smaller consequences to the credibility of the message. Therefore, it is obvious that the role of Pastor/teacher has a much greater impact on the perception of the faith, by those outside the faith. Since it may give another reason for some to avoid the question of eternity, those who are looking for excuses not to consider the implications of the claims of Christ. Those who resist the moral expectations of being a Christian. Those who desire to continue their lives uninterrupted by the sexual limitations inherent in the Christian faith. They would see the hypocrisy of leaders of the faith, and have an excuse for not exploring the truthfulness of Christianity. Without this knowledge, they may forgo the gift of salvation that is being offered to the unbelieving. Think of the impact it could have. They would reject the provision of what Christ offers, even though it is to their own demise, resulting in devastating eternal consequences. Hence, the high calling of a pastor comes with higher standards. Even for those outside the body of Christ, the high calling of a Pastor/teacher is expected by the Lord. Because eternity for someone could depend on the integrity of the person proclaiming the message. If the person proclaiming the message is not credible, then maybe the message he proclaims does not have credibility. Again, see the letters of 1 & 2 Timothy and Titus, by the Apostle Paul, for some of these requirements.

Another reason why God has such high standards for Pastor/teachers is the impact on those within the body. It can cause disillusionment for many. Particularly, those who cannot separate the truthfulness of Christianity, with the sometimes shameful behavior of those who claim to be Christians. So, for example, if a Pastor is caught having inappropriate relations outside his marriage, it undermines everything he has taught. Those who hold the Pastor in high esteem may be disheartened by his failure to live what he has taught. Should temptation take down a Pastor? That failure does significant damage to the proclamation of the truth. It affects the noble truth of everything the church should stand for. It discredits the truth. Even though the veracity of the faith remains true. Paradoxically, the foundations of the faith are true, even if the one proclaiming it does not live up to the high expectations of the calling. The negative impact of moral failure is strongly felt by believers and nonbelievers alike.

Yet, regardless of how we practice our faith, the truthfulness of Christianity, is still the truth. Take for an example, you go to the doctor and get your physical. The doctor then sits down with you and reviews your health status. He sees your weight creeping up. He reports that you're getting close to pre-diabetes. He suggests you exercise more and lose some weight. He is likely correct in His recommendations. Let's suppose that the doctor giving you the advice is overweight himself. The truth of what he is suggesting is still true even if he is not practicing the advice himself. This is true of Christianity too. The truth of the faith remains. It is true! But those poorly practicing the faith are not the best representatives, nonetheless, the truth of the faith remains just the same. That is one of the reasons why God places such high standards on those who claim the name of Christ, particularly Pastors. It affects the possible reception of the message and/or disillusions those who are part of the body of Christ. As noted, it may provide the justification for some to forgo exploring the solid evidence that validates the gospel message, even to the demise of their own eternal destiny.

Additionally, it is more than just the credibility of the message, it undermines the desired holiness that God expects for the body of Christ, particularly from the leadership. Any compromising moral failure brings old fashioned shame to everything the church is called to be, a beacon of light. The standard of truth. Accordingly, we should expect those who are called by the name of Christ, to exhibit lifestyles that are holy and upright. It is even greater for those outfront, as the face of the faith, in the role of pastor/teacher/leader. Because a compromised church is a worldly church. Exactly what we are seeing today in our church communities. A church that has lost a sense of high moral standards that should naturally be reflected in the lives of believers. Too often influenced by the standards of society around us instead of the scriptures. The standard that is described in the scriptures and not by a morally collapsing society. How can we be the salt and light in a compromised lifestyle? Keep in mind, as we stand for these principles, we should expect push back. Since, what we should stand for, will not always be a desired message from those outside the faith, and sadly, from many in the faith.

This is in line with the theological perspective that my wife and I have discussed. I think at times because it is concerning to her. She has noted some solid Christians lives fall apart. Resulting in a fearful mindset that when we step out in faith to make a difference, and live authentic Christian lives, we become a target of the enemy. Clearly, Satan wants to do us and our testimony damage. He will go after those that are making the greatest difference. That should be expected. If you step out in faith to make a difference, beware, you become a target. Should John Q, who is inactive in ministry be overtaken by a moral failure, there is a limited impact on the message. But those in leadership, and who are trusted and admired, if they fall, the impact is much more substantial. Satan has his targets. This understanding of spiritual warfare can create fear, as it has in many Chrisitian's lives. This is why many back away from the full commitment to the faith. It is easier to go with the flow.

Likely why the lukewarm believer is mostly left alone. He is not going to lose his salvation, since they are only making a limited impact with their spiritual gifts, they are little threat to this worldly kingdom. Since they are not making much of a difference anyways, Satan is not going to awaken a potential sleeping Lion. They have no interest in leading others to Christ, thereby changing the eternal destination of those who may receive the message. They are generally good people with whom you want as neighbors. They will not make people uncomfortable by witnessing. They falsely believe their character is their testimony. Behavior gives some credence to their faith, but so does the behavior of many other non-Christian faith traditions. It is the evidence that Christianity is true, that makes what we believe and share of such great value. Good neighborly behavior does not explain the gospel. They are good people, but their lives have little eternal changing value. Their impact, or lack of, will be personally felt at the Bema Seat when they realize they wasted their lives with personal pursuits, and not the causes of Christ.

This is why the calling of a Pastor is so crucial. Many have a noble desire for spiritual leadership, but lack the mature stable faith that is expected in such a role. That is why the new to the faith are not to be put into such high calling positions. (1ˢᵗ Timothy 3:6) They may have been successful in secular life, but this does not qualify them for ministry, since they are ill equipped for the coming spiritual attacks. Since Satan wants to do damage to the cause and message, and knowing the individual weakness of believers, he attacks where vulnerable.

I have been in jail ministry with those who surprise me with their depth of knowledge. But they are inmates. I believe many are really believers. They just have fresh weaknesses that do not allow them to be leaders. Some have even wanted to take over my class with their degree of knowledge. They feel this knowledge elevates them to such a role. I welcome them to participate but not dominate. In my judgment they do not have the standing credibility to be preaching or teaching. They first need to establish their long-term spiritual stability to be worthy of such a calling. There is a humbling and a mastering of the fresh that needs to take place beyond just knowledge of the Bible. Also, there are established leaders that have been vetted. We needed to be endorsed by our home church as having good standing, and go through a background check, showing we are trustworthy to be in a secure setting. This gives us recognized credibility to be involved in ministry.

Additionally we had an established well respected organization that gave leadership to this ministry. That too, gave credibility to those who taught, with each pod leader having the freedom to teach as they felt the Lord leading. It is also my personal credibility that gives me the standing to be a teacher. Those well versed in the scriptures, but not having the established righteous foundation (being inmates), need to focus on growing, not just in knowledge, but character too. Should they develop that high moral character, they most likely would not be in jail in the first place. There was one individual in particular who was very impressive with his Biblical knowledge. Rattling off scripture verses after verse only to indicate how many times he has been incarcerated. Hard to see his credibility to be a teacher of righteousness, even though he was well versed in the scriptures. The scriptures are clear, we need to be practically righteous, to have credibility to preach others, the spiritual principles of the scriptures. Since knowledge alone is not the only criteria for being in position to teach. There is necessary, and recognized credibility, to have this privilege to teach. This is crucial not only for the credibility of the gospel, but because of the coming Bema Seat judgment. If one desires a high calling, he should also be aware of the higher standards.

This is why an understanding of the Bema Seat is so very crucial to our motivation as Christains. If there were no Bema Seat, then why trouble ourselves with spiritual conflict, other than the salvation of my loved ones! Let the world go to Hell, and enjoy one's life. This is what is called Reductio ad Absurdum. It is the natural logical outcome of the faith being true but not doing anything with that truth. If there is no accountability one day, and I am not expressing authentic Christian love by sharing my faith, that is the end result of my lack of action, and the faith being true. (Not as a recommendation) This is the outcome of trying to maximize one's personal comforts and ignoring the eternal. If the desired goal is the American dream form of Christianity? Then this reasoning makes sense, the ad absurdum. Sadly, this is the practical ramifications of what is being practiced in most churches today. If you are not interested in sharing your faith? The practical truth is that you are letting people go to Hell while pursuing your personal quality of life. Be clear there will be accountability one day. It will be determined by our adherence to the list above by Hixson and Fontecchio, and chronicled by many others like Harlan Betz in his book, Setting the Stage for Eternity, and in Erwin Lutzer's book, Your Eternal Reward. Living an authentic Christain life can be sacrificially tough, but the rewards are out of this world. It ultimately comes back to the question of whether what we really profess to believe, is fundamentally true, or not.

In any war there are casualties, especially if we are not prepared for the war. We need to have the mind of Christ. To be prayed up and abiding in Christ. Actually, we must be abiding to be fruitful for Christ. This is discussed in many places, but particularly in the Gospel of John, the 15th chapter. The fruit comes not from our own effort, but by abiding with Christ, so His fruit can be produced through us. (Also discussed in chapter five of Galatians) Where we need to be walking according to the spirit to produce good spiritual fruit in our lives. This is further illustrated in Mark, chapter 4 verses 19 and 20, where the quality of the ground determined the fruitfulness. (It is not the message but the ground that determined the results) There some believers were more influenced by the cares of this world, the deceitfulness of the riches, and the ground became unfruitful. But there are also warnings, if we draw back from living out the faith, then we are like those whom the writer of Hebrews was addressing, in which God was not pleased. I understand it is natural to draw back. We all do to some degree. However, how we live does have eternal consequences. For the believer, what degree of reward is determined at the Judgment seat of Christ. Who does not want to hear from Christ, well done My good and faithful servant. What a compliment to receive at the end of life's journey.

As to what the rewards are and how long they last, there are many perspectives. Some think they last only for the 1000 year rule of Christ.

Others believe they last throughout all of eternity. This subject is worthy of full books. Some of which I noted or suggested in the suggested reading section. Others address the subject as part of their books. My emphasis is limited to the overall theme of this book. The immutable holiness of God and how that is manifested in our practical lives, and the eternal ramifications of how we lived. It is crucial to understand that we will be held accountable, and our present actions matter significantly, both now and into eternity. It is significant because of the rewards we receive for our faithfulness and/or the souls of those we led to Christ. Therefore, this teaching is worthy of our serious reflection, not only for our own benefit, but for the souls for whom Christ died. To respond in a positive manner shows we truly have an eternal perspective of life. And therefore, it is eternally profitable to endevor to live in such a manner that honors our Savior. Furthermore, there is coming a day when He will honor us as His children, for our faithfulness. While it is clear there are rewards, there are warnings too! See the next chapter.

There are many Christians who seem to coast through life with many temporal blessings and relatively few problems. As a newer believer, who has tried to be a difference maker, that too did not make much sense. It was not until I came to understand this fundamental teaching that this insight came alive. It opened my mind to the fairness of God. And that insight does not take place until we take this teaching seriously, that there are eternal rewards for our faithfulness and sacrifice. And that insight grows when we have an epiphany, a "Come to Jesus" moment regarding the horrors that await the unbeliever. When we grasp these insights, a willing sacrifice makes sense, like winning souls for Christ. But be prepared for some spiritual war in the process, so stay on your knees.

And this all makes sense if we take spiritual warfare seriously. The enemy is not going to waste a lot of time on someone who is passive in their faith. Those who take this road of comfort and ignore the eternal ramifications of the very faith we profess. Always be mindful that eternity is dependent on what we believe, and to those we witness to, what we share. This is the central truth of the Christian faith. If we choose the comforts of this world we will miss the rewards for sacrificial faithfulness. Which I believe lasts into eternity, but even if it is only for the 1000 years of Christ's rule on this earth, it will be well worth the sacrifice, as has been discussed.

A desire for good evaluation is a key factor in pleasing Christ. This is not in inorder to become a Christian, but the desired results of being His faithful child. Just as I desire certain behavior from my own children and grandchildren. It is not some status to achieve to be my children, but desired because they are my children. They will always be my children/grandchildren. Just like I am always and forever my Heavenly Father's child. This by being born again and adopted into the family of God. My faithfulness does not determine eternal sonship but it does affect eternity. The questions remain; am I as a son, walking in fellowship and obediently with my heavenly Father? Is my life a witness to the goodness of God's grace? Did I love enough to give up some comforts in this life to be rewarded in the next? Did I endeavor to reach the lost? This is also an indicator of how strongly I believe what I profess. All aspects of our lives will determine our degree of rewards, but never our salvation!

Therefore, always keep this in mind, this is not a heaven or hell question. If it were, it would lead to merit based salvation requirements, which undermines the very redemptive work of Christ, and removes the confidence of our salvation. Which further diminishes our joy, our hope, and our motivation to serve as an expression of His love.

The more the church, as a body of believers, drifts from the understanding of the immutable holiness of our heavenly Father, His ultimate justice, His fairness in all things, and the coming rewards for faithfulness, the more irrelevant we become to the world. We lose the central reason for the hope we are called to share with the world.

It remains the same question; either Christianity is fundamentally true, or it is not?

Mini Bibliography

1. Betz, Harlan D. *Setting the Stage for Eternity,* Falcon Publishing LTD, 2005
2. Beware Paul N. B*elievers Payday,* AMG Publishers, 2002
3. Lutzer, Erwin W. *Your Eternal Reward,* Moody Press, 1998
4. Numerous others as listed in sections of my Bibliography
5. Hixson, J.B. and Fontecchio, Mark, *What Lies Ahead,* Lucidbooks, 2013

CHAPTER 22

Fatherly Discipline

There is another scriptural teaching that is unknown to most Christians, denied, or not understood. It is not understood because it is not being taught. But the truth is, God our Father, disciplines His children. Likely another reason God is described as our Heavenly Father. Since He becomes our Abba Father at the moment of salvation. From the earliest chapters of the Bible, God disciplines His children. He judges the world of unbelievers. He disciplines His children because we are His children. A big difference. Judging is an exacting of a penalty for sin. It is an upholding of His righteousness. There is a penalty for sins and it must be administered to remain faithful to Himself. Some of those punishments came in time, like the flood, or Sodom and Gomorrah, when He could no longer tolerate the degree of sin on earth. Other forms of punishment and/or discipline came as God determined it was necessary for Him to intervene.

For those outside the faith, the actual individual eternal consequences start at death. (See Luke, chapter 16) Later, the final individual consequences of sin will be dealt with at the Great White Throne Judgment, when exact personal sins are judged. And the final administering of the ultimate and horrifying consequences of personal sin takes place, the eternal separation of those outside the redemptive work of Christ, into Hell. Described as a Lake of Fire. Where each unsaved man and woman will be judged as unworthy, and fairly judged, as to degrees of punishment in Hell. Even in Hell the punishment is appropriate to the degree of sin. Because God is immutable, He therefore, was unable to forgo what is required to uphold His absolute righteousness. The punishment of sin is actually a magnification of God's holiness. He is perfect in justice because He is perfect in being. Even God cannot change that aspect of His nature just because He loves, as has been discussed throughout the book. There is no subject I dislike more than this topic. However, this is one of the compelling reasons why I wrote this book. I felt the gravity of this subject was so neglected by most Chrisitans, that it needed to be explored. I reluctantly perceived that we as a body of believers needed to come to grips with this truth, no matter how vexing it is to accept.

However, the disciplining of His children has a different purpose. His anger for sin has been appeased so He no longer needs to punish us for sins. He satisfied that need on the cross at Christ's expense. We are now members of the family of God. Children of our Heavenly Father. Citizens of heaven. Therefore, He disciplines, but does not judge us. This is the consistent pattern throughout the Old Testament. And, is further developed in the New Testament. In the Old Testament, when He blessed His chosen people, included with those blessings, were warnings. His revealed expectations for ambassador living. They were to be holy people set apart to their God. The Priest of God to a world that did not know Him. It was God's means of revealing himself to the world. Which He did in various ways and through various means. As discussed in the book of Hebrews. (I would like to suggest a book by Dwight J. Pentecost, Faith that Endures. For a more thorough study of this subject)

To His own, He made clear what He expected, and as they normally did, they walked in disobedience. He would send prophets to warn them. Most prophets were faithful to the call, but often ignored. Others, like the Kings, were often a great disappointment. As usual, they walked according to the ways of the nations around them, who were notoriously wicked. After repeated warnings, He brought significant discipline upon them, even sending them into bondage by empowering Godless nations to extract the necessary discipline. Consider that as a nation who is turning our backs on God! I know we are not God's chosen people, but we were a God honoring nation, all the way back to the earliest stages of our history. An imperfect nation, but generally, a God fearing nation. Like David represented in the Old Testament, a man after God's heart, but who engaged in some serious sinful behavior.

He also dealt with individuals. Think of Moses. There is a major covenant called the Mosaic Covenant named after him. Yet, when he lost his cool, God did not allow him to enter the promised land. Moses was allowed to see, but not enter the promised land, even after being mostly faithful in his leadership. Another major covenant is named after David, the Davidic covenant. This great man of God, David, fell into a sexual sin. He tried to cover up his actions, by setting up Bathsheba's husband to be killed, a man who was faithful in his service to the king. Nevertheless, despite his greatness in the chronicles of Biblical hisotory, remember the consequences for David, after the adultry and the set up murder. God struck the infant son of David and Bathsheba to death. Then toward the end of David's life, pride got the best of him, when David counted the strength of his kingdom, against the advice of his advisor. In this particular case, God granted David the choice of chastisement. (2nd Samuel chapter 24 and 1st Chronicles chapter 21) Think of Samson and the violation of his Nazirite vows. His disobedience cost him to lose both his eyes and power. Think of Nebuchadnezzar in Daniel. It is not likely Nebuchadnezzar was a child of God, but he is a good example of both punishment and discipline. His prideful attitude angered the Lord. Then the Lord punished him. Humbling him to live and act like an animal, until he repented, and was later restored by God. He was also a tool God used to discipline His chosen people. Both are illustrations of God exacting a penalty for sin, for disobedience and pride. If God disciplined these individuals, don't think for a moment that we are beyond His firm hand of discipline. If God will discipline two of the greats in the Old Testament, what will He do to you and me, if we walk in disobedience?

This same theme continues with His Saints (all believers are positionality Saints) in the New Testament. Those who do not believe our Father is a disciplining Father need to reread much of the New Testament. The sin unto death in 1st John, chapter 5, as an example. Apparently, there were individuals who stepped over the line of God's tolerance, and were judged with the ultimate temporal judgment, premature physical death, but not the loss of salvation. Think about the sickness brought upon the Corinthians for carnal behavior in chapter 10. Where Paul uses examples from the Old Testament, of God's stern discipline, as warnings to these disobedience New Testament believers. Then he warns these believers to expect similar consequences should they continue in sin. There also is an expression of His loving discipline, as detailed in the book of Hebrews, chapter 12. The confort, if there is some, is that what the Father does, is done in love. With the purpose of correcting wayward children so they return to the path of righteous living. His Fatherly purpose of disciplining love is like any good father, the development of Godly characteristics. There are numerous other examples that could be given in both testaments. The point is, our heavenly Father is a real dad, and dad's discipline. This discipline is the desired goal of all good dads, they want their children to reflect those same first-rate qualities of righteous living.

Other times, the actions of God are more related to pursuing the sancitying of His children as through fire. The bring of doss to the top to remove what is holding them back. It is the process of purifying them for greater service. He sometimes needs to purify His children to be useful in certain services. This is not so much a discipline, but a purification of His saints. It may look the same to the believer. Just as a coach pushes an athlete to develop greater use of skills, God will sometimes use trouble and hardships to grow His children for greater use. By allowing them to experience tribulations and hardships. To break the lures of this world. These actions may not be the results of a particular sin, but God being interested in preparing us for the greater good, and His glory. The Apostle Peter and the Apostle James, both talk about this in their books. They write that the enduring of suffering matures us. They used the greatest example, Christ Himself being God in flesh, yet even He suffered, even though He was without sin.

From the beginning to the end of the Bible, the scriptures are clear, God will eventually punish sinners, in eternity, or in time and eternity. He must hold true to Himself. For the child of God, He disciplines. The difficulty is evaluating when we are being disciplined, being matured, or when it is just living in a fallen world. This may not always be known. It takes wisdom and spiritual insight. Even then it is not always clear. The first question I would ask myself is whether there is a known sin in my life that needs to be confessed and forsaken. Have I started down a path that will bring untold trouble and regret into my life? This may be God's warning to stop before the inevitable happens. When what we are doing may bring our testimony into compromise, expect God to act! Or, if our actions may bring harm to the cause of Christ, God our Father likely will be dealing with us. And it will likely be something we could or should have avoided. God is a jealous Father. A rod to the backside is often well deserved and has an intended purpose. He desires our development of practical righteousness, which is His divine purpose for all His children. Furthermore, He is serious that those who proclaim His message, model it with their behavior. God despises hypocrites. Read the Gospels on how Jesus interacted with the hypocritical Pharisees of His day.

There are eight causes of trouble in our lives as believers

1. It could be divine discipline. The main topic of this chapter. There were countless ways God disciplines His children in the scriptures. Sometimes shocking harsh discipline. Think of Ananias and Sapphira in Acts, chapter 5. It was a small lie. Yet, it appears that the movement of the Holy Spirit was so powerful, that any entrance of selfish compromise would diminish the movement of God. In another situation, the Apostle Paul turned someone over to Satan to teach him a lesson. This is seen in 1st Corinthians 5:5, when he turned someone over to Satan for the destruction of the flesh, so his spirit may be saved on the Day of the Lord. God may use Satan and/or his minions, to extract the discipline He desires to have us endure. This is seen in the Old Testament too. In 1st Samuel, particularly chapter 16, where God removed His Spirit from King Saul, and sent an evil or distressing spirit upon him for disobedience. God may also choose some form of hardship like physical pain, financial setbacks, or loss of some blessing. Or, the removal of other cherished things from our life, that we desire more than Him. There are many examples that could be included, as forms of divine discipline. We will all face some discipline in our lives. Not to experience discipline could mean you are not really His. Since the book of Hebrews indicates that being disciplined is a sign of sonship. Be sure, God will find you out for the hidden sins of your life. It is called omnisciences. He knows everything, and Dad's discipline their children! This leads me to think about the late gifted apologist Ravi Zacharias. I don't have

God's revelation on this, but I may have His mind on this. But I wonder? Could Ravi's chronic pain and sudden death be the hand of discipline from our Heavenly Father? If it was? It is a shame. He was one of the most gifted men I have ever listened to. God was using him greatly, but his flesh got the best of him. If David and Moses were subject to harsh, but deserved discipline! Don't fool yourself by playing with sin. God knows and it will cost you! I would add, it appears that God's harsh discipline is more likely for the outright rebellious, than the struggling. If you willfully defy God, believing He will not act, expect harsher discipline. (1st, Corinthians 5:5)

2. It could be the maturing process that God desires us to endure. Just like training an athlete for the sports contest, or a soldier for battle, God may be training us for the spiritual game of life. (See 2nd Timothy) Our Heavenly Father may be preparing us for some present or yet unknown situation coming into our lives, but we are not prepared for the call that is coming. An unknown ministry that he is preparing us for. But one for which we need to learn to depend on the Holy Spirit for the power of God to be equipped. Or it could be the need to remove some fleshly stronghold that is holding us back. He might be preparing us, so we will be successful for the ministry we are going to be called to undertake. Championship teams or athletes don't become such unless they are fully trained. They need to be masters of their own facilities. Spiritual training is maturing us for the coming calling. Included in this is the idea that pressure and tribulations are often designed to create tough and deeply mature believers. Some of the most deeply anchored believers are those who have endured tremendous oppositions in life. There is a desire for spiritual maturity, that God our Father has for all of us, no matter how untasteful it is to experience. (Deuteronomy chapter 8)

3. Spiritual battle. The scriptures are clear that we have an adversary that desires to destroy us, or destroy our testimony. It may come in the form of a direct spiritual attack. An attack on our mind or body or family. Whatever he wants to try to ruin. Whatever he can use to stop us in our service for the Lord. Or, through temptation, that has

the same effect. It destroys our witness through the lure of sin. Another option for Satan, he may tempt us with greed for money or power, the bitterness of the heart, or resentment. Anyway he can, he wants to destroy us. He cannot take our salvation, but he can mess up our personal lives, our family life, and nullify our salvation testimony. I would note that we are more likely to endure these attacks if we are difference makers in life, particularly, evangelistically. Satan knows once saved, always saved. That our eternal salvation is untouchable. But destroy your testimony and he stops the effectiveness of your witness.

I believe this is the avenue that he uses on many Christian leaders, the temptation of sexual sin. It starts as a little indulgence to escape momentarily the challenges of life. Before you know it, he has you in the grips of despair, and has destroyed most everything you have stood for. The cost will be far more than you ever expected. The hurt is beyond what you ever expected. You will be bewildered at how it all unraveled. I know of many very effective and good Christian men that did not respond to God's warning. It appears they fell by the allure of Satan, and they did not respond to the warning discipline. We all know that sex is very enticing. (That is why the media uses sex to sell) Who has not enjoyed this wonderful gift of God. But it needs to be kept in God's boundaries. One man and one woman for life. Or, Satan will open a door to destruction. So don't open the door!!! Keep your thoughts pure, because that is where it starts, in our minds.

4. Our troubles may simply be our own foolishness. If I get drunk and drive my car into a tree breaking my leg that is not God's doing, it is consequences for stupid! God is sovereign, but has free will figured into the plan. Sometimes my consequences are just the doings of my own foolishness. This is where the scriptures are so helpful, particularly those of Proverbs. Godly wisdom saves a lot of trouble, and maybe a broken leg!

5. Our struggles may be the results of God keeping our lives in check. I am thinking of Apostle Paul and his thorn in the flesh. He did not

do anything sinful that necessitated divine discipline. His thorn was given to cause him to be more dependent on the presence of God for his strength. God had given Paul special divine revelations that may have caused him to exalt himself with that knowledge. The thorn was allowed to remain to keep him humble and grounded. God's grace was to be sufficient for his calling. Otherwise, Paul may have gloried in his natural ability, special revelations, and not God sustaining grace.

6. There are times when even good people touch God's glory. I am thinking of 1 Chronicles, chapter 13. The Israelites were moving the Ark of God and it became unsteady. Uzzah placed his hand on the Ark to steady it, and was instantly killed. Even David was angry at God for what appeared to be overly harsh discipline. But there are times that God's glory is such, that any intrusion, results in immediate divine discipline. This is not normative, but does reflect how God feels about His glory. This is why Pastors need to be sure that their ministries are focused on giving the glory to God and not to seek their own exaltation. Like so many TV televangelists, who are too full of themselves.

7. The Federal Headship. This principle also applies in salvation history. In Adam we all inherited a sin nature. Those in Christ have been granted imputed righteousness. The headship often determines the representative results. (See Joshua chapters 7 and 22, and Judges 2;13-20) God may allow extracted consequences due to the moral choices of leaders, like in the Old Testament. When God's leaders committed sins against His revealed will, God often extracted punishment beyond just those who sinned, as in the case of David. (2nd Samuel, chapter 24) David's sin led to the death of thousands, even though they had no participating actions of their own that contributed to the consequences. The principle is also applied to the government. When a President or leader makes decisions for the people, like entering a war, it is the people who generally pay the consequences of the decision. Or, in communist or Islamic countries, where persecution comes just for holding a particular set of beliefs that are contrary to the dictates of the leadership. Think of Hitler and the results of his venomous hate of

the Jewish people. Consider that the next time you vote. If you think God will stay His hand of discipline forever, you will likely be shocked when He does act. Our country may be getting very close to needing God's harsh discipline! It may be close to the time that He separates us from our prosperity and restores our righteous foundations. Harsh discipline does that!

8. The clear fact is we live in a fallen world. The world can be a very evil place to live in. We can be the innocent victim of a crime or happenstance, or even a random, but tragic event. I work in the criminal justice system. There are a lot of evil opportunists who are on the lookout for their next victim. Many Christians were born into a world that is not favorable to the Christain faith, and being faithful, they suffer for simply loving the Lord. This also blends into the category of spiritual warfare. The list could go on and on. It is not necessary to describe them all. It is common knowledge that this world is not too friendly to believers and nonbelievers alike. Oftentimes for different reasons. But negative and very painful events come to some of the best of us. See my next chapter on suffering.

(My reflections) The alternative is also true. If we are compromising with sin, and life is going well, it may be that demonic forces have deceived you. You may have been seductively entrapped, and you are being lured into destruction. The fact that there are no presenting troubles, that normally come the way to all engaged believers, is you have been caught in deception. Sinister forces have you ripe for the destruction of your Christian faith, your family life, or the ruining of your testimony. Satan's minions may even lessen our distresses so we continue down this path of ruin. Giving you a reprieve from the stresses of life through secret sins. This lurer gets stronger and stronger until you are ruined. Satan is very deviant. Whatever works. He is glad to use the lure of sin for your spiritual demise. To draw you away from your God given walk of faith.

I have this suspicion that this is the path that ruins many men of ministry. When one engages in ministry they naturally engage in spiritual warfare. Particularly, if they are active with sharing the gospel or pro-life causes. The warfare can be intense. I wonder if the reprieve of the warfare is given to the men who finds some relief of stress by engaging in secret sexual sin. They escape then are destroyed by the escape. There are other areas that can be tempting too, like the greed for wealth or fame. Leaders may feel that they are not being properly compensated for their work, and undertake illicite, but regretful actions. This is why a firm understanding of the Bema Seat is needed. We will get paid, but it may not be until the Bema Seat. Be warned of these seductive lures of Satan. Satan's agents may back off the warfare and entice with temptation. This leads down a path that is only a temporary reprieve. One that ultimately leads down a path of destruction. Deception to destruction.

This is one of my concerns in writing a book of this nature. I have to ask myself if I am ready for what may come my way via spiritual warfare. If what I am writing is true, I anticipate, this will bring about spiritual tribulations. If the gospel does change forever the destiny of one's soul, what greater target could there be, than the one who is sharing this good news. I don't think a book that lays out a clear understanding of the way to eternal salvation, and the principles of spiritual life, is going to be well received by the enemy of our souls. Think of the evil of the holocast if you think Satan is pansy. I personally need to be sure I am walking closely with my Lord. The Devil is not my or your playmate, but a deciever and murderer, who wants to destroy us, and our testimony.

Mini Bibliography

1. Kendall, R.T. *Once Saved, Always Saved.* Authentic Media, 2005
2. Swindall, Charles R. and Zuck, Roy B., *Understanding Christian Theology,* Thomas Nelson Publishing, 2003
3. Unger, Merrill F. *What Demons Can Do To Saints*, Moody Press, 1991
4. Numerous others as listed in the recommended reading section.

CHAPTER 23

Living with heartache and confusion

It is evident that many aspects of the Christian faith are bewildering, suffering and pain for example. Unanswered prayer is another. The understanding that God can, but sometimes does not, is a bit mystifying to me as a believer. I have many issues of concern that I have soaked in prayer, and yet, I have not received my desired answers. I was up in the hospital when my best friend lost his infant daughter. One of the most generous people I know. Also, one of the most evangelistic too. Even now, more than 30 years later, the memory can still be a source of heartache. My dear wife lost her best friend to Covid. We all prayed to no avail. One wonders where God was in those times. Sometimes, I am too honest with expressing my feelings, but maybe I am saying what others will not, but are thinking privately. There is always a danger that one may get so angry they want to wave their fist in God's face. I have experienced that feeling too. It is not good. Sometimes we feel what we feel. Just being honest.

Let's look at suffering. It is almost unfathomable the amount of suffering in this world. It can be contemplated on a broader perspective, or as an individual experience. It has been the felt experience by many that God must not care. That He is indifferent to our suffering. That is a hard thought to maintain. Since it does not line up with the nature of God. At least from what I know about His revealed nature. He is a good good God! Others believe God is unable to do much about the situation at the present time, it is just a part of living in a fallen world. If that were the case, it would mean God is not sovereign. The idea that God is not sovereign is not an acceptable answer either, nor a Biblical teaching. Just look up the word sovereign as it relates to God.

The aspect of fairness is difficult to grasp too. Why are some born in circumstances, be it favorable or calamitous, with no moral contribution of either good or evil on their part. I see the good die young and those in the criminal system that are perpetual and long living predators. A continuous threat to our safety, and drag on society. It is surprising how many older men are engaging in deviant sexual behavior. Figure that out for me if you can. There are a few books in the Bible that shed some light on the subject of suffering. If you are interested, read the books of Job and Ecclesiastes in the Old Testament, and Peter in the New. But even there, a careful reading does not really give all the satisfying answers. It acknowledges the mystery of the surmised unfairness, but no real soul satisfying answers. At least from a human perspective. Some aspects of life are just a mystery to me. Let me give a few thoughts on the subject of suffering and pain. But to be clear, there are no real soul satisfying answers to the problem. There are logical answers, but few satisfying emotional ones. At least ones that fully answer the problem of evil and the pain being experienced. I am just trying to put some of these thoughts into some perspective.

The experience of pain can be in the feelings of betrayal or an unintended mishaps. It can be a significant injury or birth defect. Or, injustices that result from being victimized. Regardless of its source, those who suffer, are suffering. Regardless of the source of pain, it is real, and very personal. It is often unexplainable and unjustified in our minds. How do we make sense of this? How is this fair? How do we make sense of the meaninglessness of what we are experiencing? Let's look at a few examples.

I like sports. I like the competition and strategy of the games. The teamwork. Individuals from various backgrounds united for a common cause. I understand at the end of the day all sports are essentially meaningless. A mild distraction from the world. At the end of the game, whether my team wins or loses, it simply does not change my life. I may even agonize a bit over my team losing. Believe me, I have been a Detroit Lions fan for years. (My editorial note. Not so much anymore with most professional sports. I don't want politics in my escape from the stresses of life time. People are welcome to engage in any cause they feel is worthy, on their time, but not mine! Since few agree on what is worthy) Most others could care less what happens on the sports field, it is unimportant to them.

Just like those who have no interest in sports, people are often just indifferent to my suffering and yours. Perhaps, because they are caught up in their own misery, therefore, focused on their own presenting issues. Maybe that is why pain is so difficult. It is so very personal. And we often suffer in silence. It is unknown to most, if not all, what many are individually enduring. It shocks us when we hear of someone's suicide and how badly they wanted to escape the emotional pain. Unknown to us the suffering they were experiencing. Or, how meaningless the world has become to them. So just escape, not keeping the finality of the decision in mind, including the pain they leave behind because of the decision. It has been said that living with pain is easier than living with meaninglessness. But pain can be almost unbearable too. Especially emotional pain. We live in a world occupied with our own life struggles, and fears, and pain. And most people don't care as much as we would like to think, as long as it does not touch them. Actually, most want to avoid those thoughts, likely because it provokes fear that these adversities may eventually touch them. They just hope it just does not strike home, so they don't contemplate what others are suffering.

Sometimes it is helpful to gain a new additional perspective on the experiences of pain. Give me a chance to reflect, and see if some of my reasoning makes sense. Consider football, and the unintended consequences of playing. An butal game. As often is the case with football, it is played with no redeeming value, just for the thrill of winning. I too have suffered injury playing that silly game. I was recently watching a news special on Alex Smith, a QB in the NFL. A professional football player playing for Washington. It was gruesome to see an injury he suffered after being tackled. It took 17 surgerys and almost cost him his leg from infections. When I saw the multiple compound breaks of his leg, it made me cringe. It was disturbing to watch. Even though I did not even experience the pain, I knew it hurt. His leg was all twisted into shapes it was not designed to be. Anyone watching the injury take place knew it was excruciatingly painful. As it was to see his reaction to the injury. It was even more painful to experience for sure. I could surmise the pain he was experiencing. So how does this relate to the theological reflection on the subject of pain? Let me explain.

Pain is universal to all mankind, but it does differ in degrees. God being omniscient knows the pain we are suffering. Just as everyone watching Smith get injured, we all knew he was in serious pain. God knows what we are going through. He cannot not know, it is part of who He is as God, you remember, omnisciences. Just like the football player, we who watched, knew it was excruciatingly painful.

God knows our pain too. What does give some comfort is that He not only knows, He too experienced pain. Think about that for a moment. This is not a God who is distant from suffering. God entered humanity and experienced real rejection and pain. He lost His legal dad as a teenager. He would never marry or live the expected normal life. He was actually born with the divine purpose to die a specific death. A purposeful death. Not just to die, but to experience the most incredibly excruciating death. The brutality of the crucifixion is beyond comprehension. But even before that, He was scourged, beaten half to death. Not only did He suffer, He did it willingly. A lot of people suffer. It is beyond their ability to resist. Christ did it by divine design. He fulfilled His mission as a fulfillment of prophecy. He had the ability to stop the butal process of crucifixion at any point. But He was on a divinely designated mission. The salvation of those that would believe and accept the benefits of the cross. If you want to question the Love of God, look at the cross.

Even more difficult to understand is what he experienced when He was separated from God the Father, while accepting the payment for our sins. For all eternity, until that point, He was in perfect harmony with God the Father. But not when it came to paying for our sins. God the Father needed this payment for sin so His righteousness would be satisfied. (Remember, propitiation) And, in the most difficult moment in His life, He was also abandoned by most of His family and closest friends. And God the Father allowed Him to suffer without rescuing Him from the experience. There was a divine plan that most did not understand. So before I raise my fist in protest, I might want to do a comparison of pain experiences. Has anything I have suffered come close to what took place on the cross. While at times we contribute to our own pain, Christ undertook a plan that was voluntarily accepted because of His love. Add a thought to magnify the situation, I suffer as a sinner in a sinful world, He suffered as the creator of the world and was without sin. Perfectly God in flesh, and yet, was willing to suffer for us. Being very God in flesh! Yet loving us enough to suffer willingly to bring us to the Father. Because that is what it took to secure our salvation, an act of sacrificial love.

Furthermore, no matter what we are suffering, it is temporary. Think of suffering in light of eternity. The scriptures do address that necessary perspective of suffering. The Apostle Paul references that in the book of Romans, Chapter 8, verse 18. Where He compares our present sufferings with the anticipated Glory coming our way. Elsewhere, we are told to consider our pain in light of eternity, and with a mindset that considers those suffering as our example, like Christ Jesus. (The Apostle Peter's letters) That is why for believers, death is a blessing. To undergo endless suffering with no hope of it ever ending would be maddening. So regardless of the degree of suffering, there is an ending. There are even blessings for us who will endure suffering for the cause of Christ. No doubt, there is pain in this world. Unbelievable pain! If the pain is for this life only, then I can rest in the eternal hope of my coming resurrection body. Because there is a day coming when every tear and every pain will be recompensed, and perfect justice will be melted out to those deserving.

Last few thoughts on this subject. The thought returns to God's holiness. His justice will be distributed to those who have dispensed injustice to others. So we should leave room for God to care for those injustices, either here, in the age to come, or for all of eternity in the Lake Fire. Never forgetting that we too were deserving of His justice, because His standard never dissipates. Always remembering that for those of us who have been redeemed, there is the sure promise of eternal hope. And hope in the Bible is an assurance it will happen.

Therefore, this is the undeniable reason to be absolutely sure that we have joined the forever family of God. So required justice, which has been satisfied in the person of Jesus Christ, is an offer rejected, and we come under that ultimate eternal justice. Eternity is a long long time. No present pain can be compared to that pending justice that faces the unbeliever. The one who insists on standing on their own merits, before the perfect justice of God, will find despair that will never end. I am not sure what will be the greatest consequence of being lost for eternity? The actual punishment for sin or the mindset that there will never be an ending to it. Horrifying even to contemplate.

These thoughts may not lessen the pain we are experiencing, but they remind us that it is temporary. I am not sure how those who reject the revelation of God live in a world so full of hopelessness and suffering. It comforts me to know that my Savior too experienced pain. He knows what I am going through. So when I cry out to Him, He knows both as a real experience, and omnisciently. Therefore, no matter what suffering I am presently experiencing, it has an end, that ends in glory. Without the hope of our salvation, we all would be without recourse in this evil world. Simply, a meaningless life, in a meaningless world, that leads to declining health and ultimately, to death. Where sex and personal achievement, may give some momentary pleasure and enjoyment, lack the sustaining reason to live with the suffering that comes to all of us. Where is that hope? It is not in the purposeless world of the evolutionalist. It is the understanding that we live in a world that has God given purpose, and ends in a promised glory, even when I don't understand all the details.

CHAPTER 24

Summary Thoughts

I know that I write while sitting on the shoulders of many greats of the faith that have enriched me greatly. I certainly do not want to take too much credit for something I did not fully conceive. Although, I am confident that most everything they produced was also advanced by the sequence of learning theology truths, that was blazed by those that precede them. They too took those seeds and enhanced their themes. In my case, I simply perceived what I considered neglect to teach the essential attributes of God. In particular, the immutable holiness of God, and its ramifications. After much consideration, I believed that this is a subject that needed greater attention. I wanted to add another voice to the conversation. I hope my study of these Biblical truths enabled me to make a contribution for the cause of Christ, no matter how small. If only one person reads, and then comes to saving faith, then the whole effort will be well worth my time.

The immutable aspect of God's nature had been weighing heavy on my mind. For some reason, the idea of God being absolutely perfect, and unable to change, was profound to me. Never able to moderate who He was in His eternal essence. That His nature was intrinsic to who He is, the Holy, immutably Holy, God! The more I pondered, the more I understood the wonders of God's plan for the salvation of mankind. The need for a permanent, and complete salvation plan, that forever altered my standing with God. It made my human efforts to measure up to infinite holiness seem rather silly, and very thankful for the promises of God. He as my Savior is my assured salvation.

These thoughts also highlighted the woeful neglect of good sound presentations of the gospel. A confusing gospel is an ineffective to save gospel. We need to be clear on the content of the gospel. It is the only hope of eternal life. The only hope! Therefore, the neglect to make this a bigger priority by individuals believers and churches is puzzling in light of eternity.

This book, hopefully, will lead us to reconsider our priorities. Too focused on the pursuit of the temporary, and too neglecting the undeniable, the eternal that is coming to all of us. This emphasis on finding satisfaction in this life, with too little regard for the next, seems to me to be a misplaced priority. That did not appear to be Apostle Paul's or the other Apostles' driving passion. I understand that from various reports from church history, 11 of the 12 apostles died for the faith. (Not sure that can be completely proven. But it is clear vast followers of Christ died for their convictions) Something moved them to sacrifice all. I suggest, the evidence of the resurrection, and the knowledge of the coming judgment, the peril the lost were facing, were the prime reasons. Furthermore, they knew their sacrifices for the cause of Christ, would be honored one day at the Bema Seat.

God is a God of justice, and His immutable holiness demanded it to be upheld, to be satisfied. I reflected on the lacked of emphasis, in many areas of the normal Christian, and non-Christian alike. In my own life too. I am sure for many different reasons. The non-believer will not pursue God forgiving grace, if he/she failed to understand their hopeless status, before an unalterable holy God. The horrors that were pending upon their death. Yet so ignored or denied as a real possibility. The gospel becomes so rich and valued when seen through these truths. That I can become a forever child of God through a simple act of faith, in the gracious offer of God, because His Son already made full and complete payment. There is no contribution needed from me, foolish to even try.

It also has tremendous consequences for the church and individual believers. Yet it is sadly lacking in the church's Sunday message. So much of what we hear is for temporary enhancement of life. Not that those are teachings that the church should neglect. Nor, is necessarily wrong in itself, it just does not seem to be the major commission of the church. The call is to make disciples who can make disciples who can make disciples.

That is God's plan for the church. (Ephesians chapter 4) Discipleship is the development of the spiritual life of individuals within the body of Christ. To bring immature and newly born babes in Christ, into mature children for the propagation of God's salvation program. To be promoters of the hope of the finished work of Christ on the cross. For what reason did He die? Not to make us happy, healthy and prosperous, but sons and daughters. This with the hope that birth into the family of God would lead us to grow into seasoned mature children. The problem is that many never grow much beyond initial salvation as new babes. They begin as babes and they die as babes. Salvation benefits may have been received as a gift, but growth is sadly lacking. Of even greater concern, is not only do some not grow, they are carnal (wordly) in their Christian lives. (1st Corinthians 3:1-3) In both cases, it is likely they want the illusion of American prosperity Christianity, or they are desiring the things of the flesh more than the things of God. They do not want to entertain the clear reality of the faith, that there is a Hell to avoid, and possible rewards for faithfulness.

This, in my opinion, is often due to our failing to understand essential truths. The failure to understand the gravity of the situation. The actual implications of what we believe. Most Chrisitains simply have never thought through the implications of what we believe. This neglect to grasp the seriousness of the faith, results in a willingness to accept a soft unbiblical message. This is sadly due to the soft pedaling of the essentials of Christianity by Pastors who want to sell the best life now thinking. They, like me, have a natural desire to be liked, and socially acceptable to those both in the church and out. Enhanced, and maybe even a little embarrassed, by the call and responsibility of evangelism, which should be modeled by all Pastors. But since the unsettling reality of God's holiness is hard to accept with its natural implications, and even harder to find the courage to proclaim, most Pastors simply avoid it. They often have a hard time reconciling the actual implications of the faith with their desires for the Christianity they prefer, so they just avoid the issue. It simply comes down to one word, Hell. So instead of advancing the message, we all shrink back from sharing the faith, it is easier to ignore the implications. When was the last time you heard a message on Hell? Yet the Bible says this is the future for the majority of humanity. Which is why world evangelism is still God's heart. And the great commission is still the great commission, which was given to the body of Christ. (Matthew 28:19-20)

We know that emphasizing the hard truth of God's infinite holiness does not necessarily create a warm fuzzy church we all prefer. But it is necessary to show the imperativeness for the sharing of the gospel. It is not for those who want a feel good message on how to find personal success. Or, understanding that discipleship, as I define it, while Biblical, is hard to impress upon the body of Christ, as the expected response to the message of truth. The duplication of discipleship. Multiplication discipleship. The spiritual maturing process is necessary for God's plan to be successful. If we are not being trained to be disciplers, we are not being equipped for the ministry God has intended for the body. (Ephesians, chapter 4, indicates this is the mission for spiritual leaders, to equip the saints for the ministry) When we are not training others in discipleship, we are simply passing on information. We are Biblically informed, but the mission neglecting. To be equipped requires a good strong Biblical foundation, and, intentional, purposeful, discipleship training ministry. As often has been used, as a descriptive expression, "A soul winning ministry". But it is generally neglected for more acceptable messages. Those spiritual enrichment messages most want to hear. Truth be told, we all naturally want that soft message. I will say it again, I shun the idea of evangelism, it is not my nature. The immutability of God's holiness troubles me, and the idea of Hell troubles me. But the faith is well attested and true! It just makes logical sense, even if I don't like some of the ramifications of it being true. There are no other options, other than walking away and ignoring its truth claims. Jesus says I am "the" way, and "no one" comes to the Father "except" through me. (my loose paraphrase) Did He tell the truth? No One! Except through personal acceptance of what Jesus Christ accomplished on the cross! As he said on the cross, "It is Finished". (Gospel of John 19:30)

CHAPTER 25

Summary thoughts, Part 2

Lying in bed one night, unable to sleep, I was thinking why I felt compelled to write on such a deep subject. This is not superficial reading. Not that it is significantly profound writing. Actually, these are many of the areas of the faith that I have wrestled with for sometime. The idea of wrestling best describes what I was feeling. I was struggling with two areas of my life and could not bring them into harmony. There was my good nature, having fun, hanging out, enjoying fellowship of family and friends, that part of my life that I really enjoy. I like a good laugh. I have found I am good at one-liners. Finding humor in the moment or contrasting ironic thoughts of life. While I am in law enforcement, which tends to draw conservatives, I have found I like a good conversation with some defense attorneys. I am sure we do not see much in common, particularly with regards to religion and politics. I just like people, and find those from different backgrounds interesting. Their perspectives are sometimes insightful. They force me to think through subjects. That is true of most people with divergent backgrounds. It is interesting to see through their eyes what I may not be seeing. So engaging in these conversations allows me to see life through a different set of eyes. I don't desire to cloud those relationships with some aspiration that I should always be sharing my faith. I desire to enjoy the relationship and conversation, without thought of their spiritual condition, or eternal repercussions of what I have written about in this book.

Then there is the whole theme of this book. The urgency of the message. That Jesus was telling the truth in John 14:6. That my Christian faith was of extreme importance. That this is a subject that was more than how to have a meaningful life, it has eternal significance. I was also becoming more aware that this journey of mine was slowly winding down. Life was escaping me and there was nothing I could do to reverse it. There were chapters of my life that would never be re-lived. These thoughts created a time of renewed reflection, so I wrote a book. A summary of years of introspection regarding many aspects of the faith. Issues of extreme importance that I wanted to record and pass on. Maybe someone may even read it? Hopeful, family and friends too. It was like a lasting spiritual will, a passing on of spiritual truths, those truths that I wanted to pass on in a permanent record, particularly for my family, my children, and my grandchildren. Some meaningful lasting legacy of my life, and my spiritual journey into these profound truths.

So where do we go with these thoughts? What to do with the dilemma? The preferred lifestyle of easy going and fun loving that fits my personality. One that prefers to ignore the hard realities of life. And then, there is the inescapable of what is true; there is a holy God, the temporary nature of life, and the contingency of our eternal destination. The ramifications of the central message of the Bible, in particular, John 14:6. Which are the exclusive claims of our Savior. The only message of hope that the world so desperately needs, the gospel of Jesus Christ. This is the dilemma, and there are three options; dilute or walk away or understand that truth is often hard to accept, but true.

Dilute

This is the choice of most churches and individual Christians. Not the avoidance of the whole subject but just water down the implication of being true. When this progresses to its natural outcome, it is called progressive Christianity. It greatly minimizes the key points that I have written about. The cross is still part of the message, but its significance is greatly minimized. In its enhanced form, it evolves into universalism, where most everyone is going to make it into heaven. Our form of Christianity is just our preferred choice. It is not until Hell is a real possibility that the cross of Christ becomes so priceless. And urgent! This elevates the whole conversation of what did Christ die for, a better life? Or, the eternal redemption of hopeless sinners?

The Christian faith is greatly diminished when we start to compromise the truth. However, I believe there are compelling reasons to believe we are on solid ground with the truthfulness of the Christian faith. It makes sense. The evidence is compelling. The person who denies the faith is like a man falling off a building and denying gravity. He may deny it, but will soon be hit with the ramifications that it is true. Upon death, the denier will find out they were horribly wrong about their assumptions. Their wishful expectations were not based on the credible message of scriptures. The Gospel truth. It is likely their dislike of the truths of the Christian faith that kept them from exploring the truth of the matter. Because they wanted the temporal pleasures of this life, those pursuits of the temporal, that caused them their soul. This is generally because there are aspects of the faith that do not agree with their desired preferences. They want a God of their own creation, not a holy one. They like the kindness and goodness of God, but not holy. They see an incompatibility of love and holiness in the God they envision.

There is an initial appearance that the attributes of God conflict with each other. Actually, they are in conflict, but God had a plan that would allow a full expression of both. Yet, harmonizing God's absolute holiness and unending love, can be hard to reconcile in our minds, without minimizing one or the other. The natural response is to dilute God's holy standards. But that is not a true understanding of who God is. The alternative is to minimize the need for personal salvation. The diluting of the need for the sacrificial payment of Christ on the cross avoids the issue. These are the major reasons I wrote this book. There is a necessary understanding that opens our mind to this tension. It is not to dilute God's holiness, but to elevate the person and work of Jesus Christ. It all comes together in God's plan of redemption. God maintains His holiness and yet found a way to show His love. He was fully satisfied in the work of Christ on the cross. It really is profound when one spends time considering its implications. So we should pause and find sweet relief from the uncertainty of life after death. Knowing that for us who are saved, that our future is secure. Having the understanding that I have been fully and eternal accepted by God the Father. To dilute this message is to nullify the urgency of the whole message. We need a full and complete salvation. An eternal redemption. This is clearly the need in light of God's immutable holiness.

Walk away

This one has appealed to me at times. Just live and let live. Forget the whole subject and enjoy the life that has been granted to me. I personally don't want to be seen as one of those radical, somewhat overly religious people. Those overly zealous religious types that make people uncomfortable with the subject of their need for personal salvation. I want to be seen as a good and likable guy. A guy people just enjoy hanging out with. So I could ignore the faith. I could walk away from the implications. I had that preferred thought more than a few times. It seems so much easier. A few beers at the local pub and enjoy the fellowship and laughter. Put these thoughts aside and just live. My life is starting to wind down, so make the best of the years I have left. We did the hard work of being parents. We have earned our pensions. We could just enjoy the remaining years of retirement with adventure and experiences. The good life we all desire. I even could remain quasi religious, but just ignore the eternal ramifications. Be spiritual but avoid the whole notion that there are rewards for faithfulness. Put out of mind that Hell is a real place of consequences for sinners, who forgo the gracious offer of a pardon, that can be found at the foot of the cross.

These preferred thoughts become unsustainable thoughts, when one starts to reflect on the repercussion of those outside the faith. While freeing the mind by ignoring the implications of the faith. The obvious is still true. There is a date with destiny for all of us. The hard reality of our eventual death, not only for me, but for everyone. Realizing that to pass by an opportunity to share this offer of salvation would be most uncaring. It would indicate that I have a greater fear of rejection than I do about their eternal destiny. This truth is agonizing to even pounder. I feel the agony of it all. It is not my personality. I really like to be liked.

I feel at times my trying to harmonize those two thoughts is futile. While I can enjoy many aspects of my preferred lifestyle, there is an ultimate reality, we all have a destiny with death. And the fact remains, we all desperately need a solution to the outcome of life after death. The moment of death will eventually come for all of us. We better not be neglectful in this decision of whom to place our faith, to exercise faith in the Person who made the full redemption available for all mankind! Not when the offer of eternal salvation has been fully paid for, and the consequences are so great. It is a simple grace offered with profound eternal implications. So thanks be to God for His indescribable gift of salvation in the person and work of Jesus Christ on the cross. Since eternity is so long, I will continue the walk, but this is an option, just not lodgical in light of eternity, nor when death is a universal problem.

CHAPTER 26

Understand that truth is sometimes hard to accept but true

Since the message is true, and it can be strongly defended with compelling evidence, the reasonable response is there is an urgency for the message to be shared. A message with the highest priority. There is no other logical alternative based on the compelling evidence. Because if it is not true, what the Apostle Paul wrote in 1ˢᵗ Corithians, chapter 15, is a reasonable conclusion. His conclusion was that if the resurrection did not happen, the alternative is much preferred, get on with life. Because any personal cost to living a sacrificial Christian life is senseless. Like he said in verse 19, "If only for this life we have hope in Christ, we are pitied more than all men". NIV. Why? Because we are living a lie. We are giving a false hope. And those who are suffering for the hope of the gospel have been deceived. Why suffer for a lie, when there are no personal or monetary benefits for doing so? Moreover, there is no reason to make our relationship awkward by imploring the unsaved to come to saving faith. Furthermore, without the resurrection, those that have passed on from this life are just gone, it is over with. No hope for the dead. Just nothingness. He continues the logic in the same chapter, in verse 32 b, that also makes deductive logical sense. "Let us eat and drink, for tomorrow we die", NIV. If we lose the hope of the resurrection, and the salvation message, then what is left? We are still going to die. Life without the hope of the resurrection is meaningless. (Yet, is that not the strongest yearning of all men, a hope when standing at the grave of a loved one, or facing one's own mortality) But without the resurrection, there is no hope! Drink a few beers and enjoy those fleeting years that remain of life. Logic dictates that maybe we even dance with the dark side of the world.

But since the Christian faith is true! There is no altering these facts! While emotionally troubling when we are pondering some of the harder aspects of the faith, it is also the greatest message ever to have been given to mankind to share. The ultimate hope! Eternity is a long long time. So the gospel message shared is the greatest act of love. It clarifies the eternal consequences of the message, the good and bad. For those who believe, the good news of our acceptance into the forever family of God. Eventually, free from the effects of sin, death and pain. The bad, if you neglect the offer, the holy standards will be satisfied by the judgment of your sin, your eternal consequences. Since your lack of personal righteousness can never measure up to the infinite and eternal holiness of the immutable God. The facts remain. People go to Hell because they have been diagnosed as sinners, and don't accept the payment made by the Savior, so they are judged as sinners. Far too much is at stake to dilute or walk away. Death is so final. The consequences are so final. Even if it is hard to accept all of its implications. This is the story of our redemption, therefore, it should become our ministry of sharing the way of redemption. Since the eternal is coming and death is final, we need to walk out of faith.

This is even manifested in the way we consider death. My friend George has remarked that God sees death differently than we do. I believe he is correct. The perspective is with the beholder. The truth of the outcome is according to the scriptures. God sees the continuance of our lives. We go from being Saints that remain in sinful flesh, even after becoming a Christian, to Saints in His presence. For the believer, the entrance of death into our lives is just the changing of location to a much better place. We leave the restrictions and sinful flesh for unfettered glorification. Which is the removal of our sinful tendencies. Finally free of sinful impulses. Free from pain and suffering. Life in the very presence of our Heavenly Father. This perspective of God's should be that of our own. Death should not be feared. Glory is our guaranteed future.

For the non-believer, it is absolutely devastating. The end of this life is the final chance for salvation. It is final! The uncertainty of what happens after death is realized. The baseless hope of meriting salvation on their own is found wanting. It is forever, too late! The eternal is set and results unalterable. Please do not put this book away until you have resolved this question of your eternal destiny.

I tried to keep the subject matter as a general deductive conclusions of key Biblical principles. If this is true, then? If not, then? I felt it was worth bringing back into focus what is often neglected in most churches. A message of eternal significance!. I have read in a couple of places that around 95% of all "Christians" never lead one person to Christ. That just does not add up with the truth claims central to the faith. Many will be disturbed by the suggested implication of the book. It is not the message they want to entertain. They like their lives. So do I! I like to be liked. It is my nature. Most likely those who do not care for the message, will be those whose lives are going quite well, or the truths of this message is too hard to accept. They don't even want to think about these matters. They are happy with their quality of life, and want to continue the illusion that it will last, it won't, I am sad to say. Each man is appointed to die one day and then a judgment. The Bema Seat judgment for the child of God. Where our lives will be evaluated for quality. The Lake of Fire for the unbeliever. Where the unmitigated righteousness of God will be revealed.

Was this book journey worth reading? I hope so. I know it is not a popular topic to discuss. But it is a message I felt that needed another voice. The bringing back into our thinking, the urgent need for the salvation of the lost. A chance to reflect once again on the implications of God's absolute pure holiness, to the attention of both the saved and unsaved. To draw attention back to the hope we can have in Christ. The coming to grips with the immutable perfect nature of God as it relates to the final judgment. In Romans, the Apostle Paul says he is not ashamed of the gospel. Neither should we, it is truly the greatest message ever given to mankind, and the greatest message to be shared. The salvific message that is professed to believe, but ignored by the majority of Christains. This is because we have a growing worldly church that is trying to find approval with the world and not from Christ. (See the rebuke of many of the churches in the book of Revelation) For those believers who are lacking in their faith walk, they need to remember that there is a day when all believers will stand before the Bema Seat of Christ. A time of reckoning on what was really important in light of eternity. For the unbeliever …. It is hard to even consider.

Since it is true, it therefore has immense implied responsibilities for the believer. To fail to respond evangelistically is a denial of everything we profess to believe. Christianity at its very core is an evangelical faith. If you do not see that it is likely your eyes are being blinded by Satan. (2 Corinthians 4:4) Therefore, one more time, it is important to consider these themes. The understanding of the immutable holiness of God, and the finality of the work on the cross by our wonderful Savior, Jesus Christ, and the coming day of judgment. The litmus test applied to the reality of life. A message of hope that is urgently needed in a hopeless world. This understanding should lead us to have a renewed priority to live more eternally purposeful lives. Hopefully, this book has stimulated a renewed interest in the eternal.

It is an eternal destination question; either it is true or it is not? It is! So get on living it!

CHAPTER 27

Walking away and coming home again

Some restorative thoughts for those who have once been part of the faith community and later walked away, and now they reflect on the aftermath of that choice. It generally starts as seeds of doubt over the truthfulness of Christianity. It is a good part of the reason so many young people are leaving the church. They have lost faith in their faith. And the church owns much of the blame. We are simply not equipping young believers in the foundations of the faith. We are pretty good at telling them what we believe, but deficient when it comes to why we believe. When challenged later in life, usually in college, they become disillusioned with what they had believed, and abandon the practical aspects of the faith. They are so ill equipped when it comes to knowing why the Christiain faith is well attested, and can be defended, and trusted, as a foundation for living. A sure foundation in a world of confusion. Without that confidence, they leave the faith, and abandon the practical practice of those values that flow from the clear teachings of the faith. They become deceived. Which leads to them becoming disenchanted with what they once were taught. They only hold on to a shadow of their moral anchor. Once the anchor is dislodged, they pursue worldly satisfaction to fill the void in their souls.

Therefore, it should be of no surprise that many leave for a season. They are no longer able to trust what had been taught to them. This is one of the deficiencies of the church not providing the grounds for that assurance. If the church made this a priority and equipped them before leaving, more would continue on in the faith, knowing their faith was well founded and relevant to real life. Otherwise, the allures of society that are presented as consequences free, often in the form of sexual temptations, will be too strong to overcome when tempted. Later, in reflection, they will realize those choices have become memories of regret, with shame and guilt as the natural consequences. And the devaluing of the sanctity of marriage bonds is the results. This is the victory that Satan enjoys, devaluing the person, marriage, and the message.

I think this is an experience that many Christians have. They were part of a stable church. Then they take a vacation from the faith, or abandon it, because of the philosophies of this world, or because of peer pressure. They indulge in sexual experimentation, then later they return to the faith, wanting to return to their spiritual foundations. Sensing that something is missing in their lives. For others, it comes when they start a family, and they want that spiritual foundation instilled in their children's lives. Then in reflection, they reassess those choices they made, with the moral expectation of the faith, and find regret and remorse as the end results. They now wished that part of the journey had been avoided. It often weakens the sanctity of the bond of marriage. Because deep down in their hearts they knew better. It devalued the sanctity of their sex lives. Sex went from a sacred union to an expereience to be explored. They thought they had found freedom, but it never was freedom. It was the temptation that led to remorse. It was giving in to the fresh. The resulting feeling is they have lost something precious because of those choices. A feeling of the loss of wholesomeness. This is a natural guilt feeling. Because they knew what it was, and what God sees, as unsactified sex. That is why that act of sex outside of marriage is regrettable. It does not have God's blessings. If this is true of you? Go back and reread this book. It really is a book of hope. It is a warning for sure, but ultimately, it is the restoring hope of the gospel message. First in ultimate salvation, and then in practical restoring salvation. A reminder that we are children of our Heavenly Father. We are clothed in the very righteousness of Christ. Then putting the Apostle Paul's instruction to use, as he wrote about in Philippians, chapter 3. Accept God's cleansing forgiveness and seeing ourselves clothed in the very righteousness of Christ. Then having that wisdom, moving on in the instructions of Paul, putting the past in the past. Forgiving ourselves and living out the redeemed life we have in Christ. Our true identity in Christ. Not allowing that regret to steal anymore of our joy and peace.

This was also the prayer of David after he grievously sinned. He did not ask to be saved again, that was unnecessary, but the joy of his salvation to be restored. (Psalms 52:12) Because when one is living in sin as a child of God, their fellowship with God is broken, and their joy is lost. Therefore, accept God's gracious forgiveness, and move forward in the restoring blessings God has for you marriage. Because God has blessed the sexual union of a married couple. Sex is intended to be a freely given expression of an sanctified union. (1st Corinthians, chapter 6:11, and chapter 7:1-7)

As part of the creative order, marriage sex is seen by God as santified sex. Therefore, it is encouraged as an healthy expression of the love that God intended for married couples. A freedom to enjoy to the max. We are even told not to withhold from each other because this is an avenue that Satan will tempt. (1 Corithians chapter 7) We are to find satisfaction in the breast of the wife. So says the Bible! (Psalms 5:18-19) This is why we need to be anchored in the strong doctrine of our faith, and put to practice the principles of the faith. This is the insight we gain by being grounded in the faith. It reveals why the holiness of God has practical ramifications now, and profound ramifications into eternity.

So, as strongly as I can, I suggest taking the time to study those who have written so persuasively on this subject. It will anchor your faith. And put your moral foundation on solid ground. (Many of those books that have helped me are included in my reading list) A sure confidence in what we believe is the result of this investment. And, may save a person from the illusions of this world, which is often manifested later as sexual regret. Then being equipped with the assured confidence of our faith, we all are prepared to be eternal difference makers. This is the desire for all of God's children, a meaningful life, that is a joy filled life! Fully forgiven and fully accepted.

CHAPTER 28

A *few last reflections on miscellaneous ideas*

Brief thoughts on ministry, our culture and jail ministry.

I don't want to dive too deep here since it would be another book. So I will limit myself to a few brief thoughts and close the cover of the book. I have spent considerable time thinking about the culture divide. We are not in a good place. There is little trust in our government, with politics being treated as though it is like sports, whatever can be done to win. We lost the foundation for truth. But the truth is the truth, even if denied. The media compounds the problem with their neglect of what is true or a simple distortion of truth. It is hard to believe much of anything they broadcast. Then there is a common theme on TV that degenerates the image and role of a husband. This is not good. We need to promote the necessity of a solid, and faithful man in the home. They are unwisely transforming our county. If someone objects to what they believe may not be helpful to our society, they are shamed for not endorsing what is often clearly sin. Simply to remark that people are statistically better when basic Biblical principles are endorsed, brings name calling. Some ....ism is the label. This without even asking if there is some valued point to the perspective. A real conversation on what is noble and good for our country is hard to achieve. The government has dug a very deep ditch of debt. No one appears to understand the cost to future generations. Few in Washington appear to want to make the hard decisions. They pass the buck to the next generation. Our young people will be stuck with our greed and our waste. Then again, they are often the ones who have been told that they should expect everything for free. The only real free gift is our salvation, and even that too was paid for. Thank You Jesus.

But think with me for a few moments. I am not saying all was well sixty years ago. The I Love Lucy, Leave it to Beaver and Andy Griffith shows period. The old black and white TV programs many of us grew up watching. Do you remember that it was inappropriate to even mention that Lucy was pregnant on the show. Compare that with the drift that we are now seeing. It is alarming. What would once shock people is normalized. This is where God's ordained model of society is so helpful. There are three primary units; the family, the church, and the government to restrain evil. Each of these complement and support the other. Have strong families and Bible teaching churches and you have a healthier society. But with the demise of the family and the compromising church you get an overbearing government. A government that now promotes evil and threatens those who say so. We have gone from the original intent of government, that government was ours, to the idea held by those in government, that we are the governments. This is a compounded problem when the government becomes promoters of evil.

Visualize this scene. A man is waiting at the altar for his bride to be. Both have kept themselves for this day. They marry with the full intent to stay so until death. The investment is the family not the illusions of personal pleasures. Respect is the norm, and is expected. Kindness permeates throughout society. Dad provides enough income to allow mom to stay home and attend to the responsibilities of the home and kids. Almost everyone attended church on Sunday. It was a true day of rest. Very few businesses were open. Only the essential. There was a general wholeness to daily living. Men would never swear in front of a lady. A lady was just that, a lady. Hard work was expected and ingrained in our children. The kids played ball down at the local park, or in our backyards, and were safe playing there. You get the picture. A very simple, more wholesome life. We should be shocked by what we are seeing, instead we accept it as the new normal. (This illustrative portrayal is not to indicate a standard for women. My wife, sisters and daughters all have successful professional careers. The point is the contrast between the changing culture)

What we now call freedom is really sexual bondage. The decline accelerated in the 60's with the removal of Bible reading and prayer in public schools. This resulted in the loss of truth and our personal awareness of our dependent relationship with God. In its place the government took the role of the dad. Women could have children without regard to many of the consequences, with the assurance that society would care for the needs. Our responses were noble in caring for the children, but that came with unintended societal declining consequences. This led to the freedom to act irresponsible and without personal responsibility. Government has failed to understand the full impact of abandoning these foundational values. Godly dads are desperately needed. Every fair study shows that the absence of a dad in the home leads to devastating consequences to the next generation. Which is then compounded to the next.

This also leads to the declining mental health status of our society. And that in itself is troubling. The problems of the lack of morality continue to manifest. The divorce rate both in and out of the church reflects the lack of commitment of the promise. This breakdown of society has led to full jails and prisons. There is way too much violence in the streets. Drug and alcohol abuse are destroying our young people. There are places in some cities where it is not safe to travel through. People killing each other for drugs or territorial imposed claims. You think we could use a little old fashioned return to wholesome morality, to Biblical standards that so many call outdated. I think we need to rethink our values and foundational standards. Some Bible reading and prayer back in schools would not hurt. Seriously! What benefit has society gained with the removal of those practices? A little old fashion wholesomeness would be more than welcome. I think we would find true freedom, and sleep better at night!

In regards to jail ministry and working in the criminal justice system, I take some pride in the fact that when I had the authority, I exercised restraint. Hopefully mixed with compassion. I mean I am a politically and religiously conservative person who did jail ministry. I am sure some of my colleagues see my ministry as fraternizing with the enemy. But a little research into the lives of many who are serving time is enlightening. They generally lack a good moral education. Many have learning limitations and/or they lack the support of a stable home. A large percent have mental health issues. In my opinion, the biggest issue is the lack of well grounded

Godly fathers in the home. This too is an indicator of the digression of our morals. These thoughts have compelled me to try to make a difference. I know I am not to the degree that I should be. Maybe my emphasis in this book will motivate me more too.

There is also the devaluing factor of what is being taught in our schools and universities. The value of life is diminished when evolution is the only theory taught. You can't teach someone that their ancestor is a monkey and then claim they are worthy of dignity. The foundation for seeing ourselves as having individual worth, is that we were created in the image of God. We have in many of our public schools that have abandoned the virtuous character building that historically built our stable society. There are still many good schools, and a growing moment of Christian schools and a homeschool movement, that give us hope. We can also see this digression when we remember that the majority of universities, in the early stages of our country, were founded as distinctly Chrisitan. They are established as highly principled and Biblically grounded, exulting the greatness of God. Those principles are now largely lost to Godless imposed viewpoints being propagated by those in control of our educational system. And generally unchallenged.

But this decline in our society also angers me. We are all paying the price for our progressively declining moral values. One starts to wonder when will people ever learn? How long does society put up with such nonsense? How long will God put up with this nonsense? Unfortunately, prison and jail do not seem to help much. It does provide some protection, but little change. (check out the recidivism rates) All at a very expensive cost of wasted human lives and significantly monetarily to the rest of society. We are broken people. Remove those moral restraints and see what happens. What is happening! The removal of these Biblical principles, for the promise of freedom, has only led to emotional and spiritual bondage. Break down those foundational morals and you see what we are experiencing. There is not enough money that can fix this situation. No sound parent would reward a child for bad choices. But the government believes we are obligated to remove all accountability. Therefore, individuals know that regardless of the choice, the government will care for their needs. It is the freedom to keep having children out of wedlock, and expect everyone who acts morally to absorb the cost. Society has resources to help, but when the system is overloaded, it collapses. Yes, we need to care for the children, but we also need some accountability too. We need a revival of traditional Biblical values or we are going to collapse. Our constitution as John Adams noted, was conditioned on us being a moral and religious people. Very little of those values are manifesting anymore. God help us!

Yet the present direction is anything but the return of good solid family values. Those Biblical values that resulted in the greatness of our country, are the same values that are desperately needed for the rebuilding of our foundations. Regretfully, the opposite is taking place as a movement, there is an acceleration into moral chaos. You cannot destroy the foundations and not expect the unraveling of our society. There are core values that hold society together, our common Christian faith for one. Even when the validity of faith was not personally held, the values that emanated from the Bible were practiced as social norms. We were not perfect, but much better off before we started this removal of the Bible reading and prayer in schools. We are now seeing a degradation of the value of life. Everything wholesome is being forsaken. This is principally due to the loss of truth, particularly the Biblical truth of the immutable holiness of God. There are consequences, to both our personal lives, and in eternity. There is only one hope, the gospel of Jesus Christ. There is only one ultimate source of ultimate truth, the Bible.

So I end this with this last thought. The question remains, is it true or not? Was Jesus telling the truth as recorded in John 14:6? Have YOU taken advantage of the offer of eternal salvation? Faith alone in Christ alone, based on the finished work on the cross alone, brings forgiveness of ALL SIN, and eternal life! Then we need to move forward in restoring righteousness, by applying those Biblical principles.

ABOUT THE AUTHOR

Steven lives in Michigan with his wife of approximately 40 years. They have three adult children and a growing number of grandchildren. He retired after a 30+ year career in various forms of law enforcement. He presently works part time in a law enforcement role. He served as Mayor and Mayor Pro-tem of the City of Port Huron where he has lived the majority of his life. He served as a Vice President of a Charter School for troubled youth. He is on a board for a nonprofit halfway program for criminal offenders. He has served on a number of other boards, both Christian and secular. He was active in coaching in the lives of his children. He served 7 years doing jail ministry and was involved in a number of other Christian related activities. His heartbeat is evangelism. This is his first attempt at a book.

There is no implied endorsement, by any association, organization, boards, ministries or employment (past or present) for this book or its content. The opinions are solely mine.

I know this was not a professionally written book. That is beyond my ability. It was a book that took these essential divinely revealed truths, and explored the significance of what the faith really means because it is true. And it may appear at times that I was babbling on and on. Yet, if I was able to make the points I wanted to make, and instilled them in the reader's memory, by repeating key truths over and over, I can live with my lack of proficient writing skills. What is important is impressing on the reader the clear implication of Biblical Christianity being true! Hope you gained some benefit from my thoughts. With that last thought, I will close the book. God Bless You!

The truth as claimed by Jesus, is still the truth, John 14:6

I do not necessarily agree with every detailed teaching in the below listed books. But I have found real value in all of them. They are all well worth reading. There are dozens and dozens more in my library, but these are enough to ground you in your walk.

BIBLIOGRAPHY

Batterson, Mark, _The Circle Maker,_ Zondervan, 2011

Betz, Harlan D. _Setting the Stage for Eternity,_ Falcon Publishing LTD, 2005

Beware Paul N. B_elievers Payday,_ AMG Publishers, 2002

Bing, Charles C. _Lordship Salvation,_ Ph.D. Dissertation, 1991

Bing, Charles C. _Simply By Grace,_ Kregel Publishing, 2009

Bing, Charles C. _Grace Salvations and Discipleship,_ Grace Theology Press, 2015

Chafer, Lewis Sperry, _Salvation,_ Kregel Publications, 1991

Chafer, Lewis Sperry, _True Evangelism,_ Kregel Publications, 1993

Chafer, Lewis Sperry, _Grace,_ Kregel Publications, 1995

Cocoris, G. Michael, _The Salvation Controversy,_ Insights From the Word, 2008

Cocoris, G. Michael, _Repentance. The Most Misunderstood Word in the Bible,_ Grace Gospel Press, 2010

Cucuzza, Thomas M. _Secure forever!_ WWW.xulonpress.com, 2007

Evans, Phillip M. _Eternal Security Proved,_ Published by Lulu.com, 2008

Eaton, Michael, _No Condemnation, A New Theology of Assurance,_ InterVarsity Press, 1995

Gromacki, Robert Glenn, _Salvation is Forever,_ Moody Press, 1973

Halsey, Michael D., _Truthspeak,_ Grace Gospel Press, 2010

Halsey, Michael D. THE GOSPEL of GRACE and TRUTH, Grace Gospel Press, 2015

Hixson, J. B. _The Gospel Unplugged, Lucidbook,_ 2011

Hixson, J. B., Whitmire, Rick, Zuck, Roy B. _Freely By His Grace,_ Grace Gospel Press, 2012

Hixson, J. B., Ge_tting the Gospel Wrong,_ Grace Gospel Press, 2013

Hixson, J.B., and Fontecchio, Mark, _What Lies Ahead,_ Lucid Books, 2013

Hixson, J. B. _Top 10 Reasons some people go to Hell, and One Reason No One Ever Has To!_ Grace Acres Press, 2020

Jones, Brian, _Hell is Real (But I hate to Admit it)_ David Cook, 2011

Kendall, R.T. _Once Saved, Always Saved._ Authentic Media, 2005

Lightner, Robert P. _Sin, the Savior and Salvation,_ Thomas Nelson, 1991

Lindsey, Hal, _Satan Is Alive and Well on the Planet Earth,_ Zondervan, 1972

Lindsey, Hal, _Amazing Grace_, Western Front, 1995

Lutzer Erwin W. _How You Can Be Sure That You Will Spend Eternity with God,_ Moody Press,1996

Lutzer Erwin W. _One Minute After You Die,_ Moody Press, 1997

Lutzer, Erwin W. _Your Eternal Reward,_ Moody Press, 1998

Lybrand, Fred *Back to FAITH Reclaiming the Gospel Clarity in an AGE of INCONGRUENCE,* xulonpress.com, 2009

Mansfield, Stephen, *Killing Jesus,* Worthy Publications, 2013

Moyer, R. Larry, *Free and Clear,* Kregel Publications, 1997

Olson, Lloyd A. *Eternal Security, Once Saved Always Saved,* Tate Publishing and Enterprises, 2007

Pentecost, J. Dwight, *The Joy of Fellowship,* Kregel Publications, 1977

Pentecost, J. Dwight, *Faith that Endures,* Kregel Publications, 2000

Radmacher, Earl D. *Salvation,* Word Publishing, 2000

Rokser, Dennis M. *SHALL NEVER PERISH, Forever.* Grace Gospel Press, 2012

Rokser, Dennis M. *Salvation in Three Time Zones,* Grace Gospel Press, 2013

Rokser, Dennis M. *Don't Ask Jesus into Your Heart*, Grace Gospel Press, 2014

Ryrie, Charles C. *So Great of Salvation,* Victor Books 1989

Shea, Ronald, Booklet, *The Gospel,* Grace Gospel Press, 1988

Stanley, Charles. *Eternal Security*, Thomas Nelson Publishers 1990

Stegall, Thomas L. *The Gospel of the Christ,* 2009

Strombeck, J. F. *So Great of Salvation,* Kregel Publications, 1991

Strombeck, J. F. *Shall Never Perish,* Kregel Publications, 1991

Swindall, Charles R. and Zuck, Roy B., *Understanding Christian Theology,* Thomas Nelson Publishing, 2003

Tam, Stanley, *Every Christian a Soul Winner*, Thomas Nelson Publishers, 1975

Tripp, Paul David *Forever, Why You Can't Live Without it*, Zondervan, 2011

Unger, Merrill F. *What Demons Can Do To Saint*s, Moody Press, 1991

Vandergriend, Alvin, *Love To Pray*, Prayer Shop Publishing, 2003

Yohannan, K. P, *Living in Light of Eternity*. Chosen, A Division of Baker Book House

SUGGESTED READINGS TO SUPPORT MY CONTENTION OF THE REALITY OF GOD AND RELIABILITY OF THE BIBLE

Ankerberg, John and Weldon, John, *Ready for an Answer*, Harvest House Publishers, 1997

Comfort, Ray, *Evolution A Fairly Tale for Grownups*, Bridge-Logos 2008

Cross, John R. *By this Name*, Goodseed, 2014

Davis, Max, *The Insanity of Unbelief*, 2012, Destiny Image

D'Souza, Dinesh, *What's so Great About Christianity*, Tyndale House, 2007

Geisler, Norman L. *Christian Apologetics*, Baker Book House, 1976

Geisler, Norman L. and Turek, Frank, *I Don't Have Enough FAITH to be an ATHEIST*, CROSSWAY, 2004

Johnson, Phillip E., *Darwin on Trial*, InterVarsity Press, 1993

Limbaugh, David, *Jesus on Trial*, Regnery Publishing, 2014

Lutzer Erwin W. *Seven Reasons Why You Can Trust The Bible*, Moody Press, 1998